SOULFUL AGING

Ministry through the Stages of Adulthood

HENRY C. SIMMONS
JANE WILSON

Smyth & Helwys Publishing, Inc.
Macon, Georgia

Smyth & Helwys Publishing, Inc.
6316 Peake Road
Macon, Georgia 31210-3960
1-800-747-3016
©2001 by Smyth & Helwys Publishing
All rights reserved.
Printed in the United States of America.

The paper used in this publication meets the minimum requirements of American
National Standard for Information Sciences—Permanence of Paper for Printed
Library Materials.
ANSI Z39.48–1984. (alk. paper)

All biblical quotations are taken from the New Revised Standard Version (NRSV)
unless otherwise indicated.

Library of Congress Cataloging-in-Publication Data

Simmons, Henry C.
    Soulful aging : ministry through the stages of adulthood / Henry C. Simmons,
    Jane Wilson.
       p. cm.
    Includes bibliographical references.
    ISBN 1-57312-346-3 (alk. paper)
     1. Church work with the aged. 2. Christian aged—Religious life.
    I. Wilson, Jane 1959–
    II. Title.

    BV4435 .S56 2001
    259'.3—dc21   00-054919

CONTENTS

INTRODUCTION

It is said that if you want to see the shape of the country in 20 years, go to Florida. Perhaps it could also be said that if you want to see the shape of Florida in 20 years, go to church. The historic, or mainline, churches have increasingly large percentages of older adults as congregants and proportionally fewer younger adults or children in the church. Their congregations are aging in place. There are three typical responses to this phenomenon: (1) wishful thinking and nostalgia, (2) desperation and despair, and (3) the belief that all of life is holy.

Responses to Aging

The first response lies somewhere between wishful thinking and nostalgia—"It would be lovely to have more children and young families like we always had, so shouldn't we get a new youth director who can bring them in?" An unintended effect of this response is that the minister ends up feeling guilt and failure: "I must have done something wrong if I haven't attracted young families." The responses of wishful thinking and nostalgia fail to take into account the dramatic shift in demographics—there are simply not enough young people to fill all our churches. Nor does it factor in the profound social changes that have swept away the familiar world in which churchgoing was taken for granted as much as Sunday store closings.

The second response to aging churches lies somewhere between desperation and despair: "We've tried *everything* we could think of, and look, we're just a bunch of old people." Often those congregations expressing such sentiments *have* tried everything they could think of. They have read, studied, prayed, done mission projects, canvassed the neighborhood, modernized the music at one of the Sunday services, or created a day-care or afterschool program. The net results are predictable: few or no new congregants and a gnawing sense of despair or even self-hatred. The worst example we have seen of this was in a small, rural, relatively affluent congregation where the youngest member was in her early 70s. In an all-congregation meeting, they discussed installing an elevator so that the increasing number of congregants who couldn't get up the 16 steps to the church would not be denied access to worship. Their conclusion was this: It would not be right to spend all that money on old people. Such age-rage turned against oneself shows the power of social norms that identify the true human as youthful looking, productive, and strong.

The third response to aging congregations is more difficult to characterize in a few words. It cannot be typified as the antithesis of wishful thinking + nostalgia + desperation + despair. It knows all these realities, but it resists them. It knows that there is no going back, that the presence of large numbers of elders in the church is a fact that will not go away, that there is no quick fix that will restore a remembered past. But above all it looks squarely into the faces of the elders and asks, with them, what in God's providence does this mean? What is God's will in this? What are we to learn from it? What are we to do? How can we, together, continue to be faithful?

Underlying the resistance to despair, there is a profound conviction, sometimes hardly articulated, that all of life is holy—not just the beginning, not just the years of youth, not just the parenting years, not just the middle years. All of life is holy. The years from retirement to death are holy—frailty included.

What is wrong with the first two typical responses may be made clearer in a story—sadly, a true story. Rob and Cara were co-pastors in a rural church for five years. Their congregants, about 80 in number, were all past age 70. Some were still close to retirement; some had gone through the death of a spouse and were sorting out a new life; many were frail; and some were close to death. Rob and Cara then moved to a large city where Cara became a hospital chaplain and Rob a director of education at an 1800-member, high-growth, suburban church. Rob was elated. "Out in the country" he exulted, "those good people just went through their routines. Here I can see real transformation day in and day out."

As we mused on this situation later, we thought, "Rob you got it backwards." In the rural church, real transformation, life and death, was happening. Unless you are in a coma, you can't just cruise through the last third of life into death without facing some of life's greatest challenges—challenges that are, at heart, spiritual. For example,

- What do you do with the retirement years?
- What legacy do you want to leave?
- How do you deal with illness or the death of a spouse?
- How do you start over when the one you most loved is gone?
- How do you face the need for help when you have always been independent?
- What do you do with frailty that may even include, God forbid, diapers?
- How do you make right what was wrong in your life?
- How do you deal with approaching death?
- How do you accept life's twilight and death's darkness?

Rob and Cara just didn't see all these parts of the journey of life as God's gifts and challenges.

What Rob did see in the adults in his new church might be transformation or development or change. The family years are not without their spiritual challenges, but they ought not obliterate the seriousness and spiritual preeminence of the challenges of later life. Indeed, we get a glimpse of ourselves in early midlife in the practice of certain devout Hindus who only embark on a serious spiritual quest when they have completed the tasks of the householder. Perhaps the simplest test of the relative weight of the two parts of the journey of your one life is to ask which part you personally would rather deal with (not that we are going to get a choice!). That question has a way of cutting through the cultural fog that sees later life as a non-event.

We are profoundly children of our culture. It is a culture that does not look kindly on old people. Old wine, old furniture, old castles—yes. Old people—no. No matter how hard we try, we still find our eyes and our hearts going to those who are youthful-looking, strong, and productive. Even when older adults are portrayed like the beautiful people of *Modern Maturity* (who, compared to us, are younger-looking, wealthier, more fit, happier), it is not easy to tear ourselves loose from our deeply embedded cultural prejudices that make us equate life with youth.

So where do we go? As a friend of ours, justly noted for her lack of pastoral skills, would say, "Just get over it!" We don't have a choice about those with whom we will minister. The church we know is, in substantial measure, an aging church. Indeed it is not an insurmountable challenge. Most of us are capable of getting to a life-stance that takes seriously that the whole of life is holy. All of us are capable of getting to the point where we can ask seriously what is God's will for this aging church, its members, and its leaders.

We don't claim this will be easy. First, our culture and church are biased towards youth. The normative human is young, beautiful, and productive. This high-noon vision of the human denies the humanness of the frail. Second, the spiritual challenges we will have to work with are substantial and serious. The struggles of the soul are holy struggles. All that is holy comes from the One who is holy. No spiritual guide steps lightly on holy ground, but enter we must. We are called to ministry as pastors, laypersons, and teachers. Our congregants—those entrusted to our care—need and deserve spiritual guidance, even if, or especially when, they are in the last third of life.

Stages of Senior Adulthood

The last third of life is often caricatured as "the good years" and "the bad years." No life is that simple. Lives in progress have challenges and delights. Like all of life, the last third is marked by periods of stability and times of transition. Understanding this reality and distinguishing these stages and phases of aging is a first step in ministry with those in the last third of life.

Here is a model of aging that distinguishes three stable periods, each followed by a transition. The model was originally developed by James Fisher, a colleague and friend. In considering this model, be thoughtful about the impact of gender, socioeconomic status, context (one's location on the metropolitan-rural continuum, along with one's family context), and cohort (the group one was born with). These variables profoundly shape the whole of life. Their impact, particularly any negative impact, becomes stronger in the last third of life.

Henry and his co-author, E. Craig MacBean, modified Fisher's model somewhat in their book, *Thriving After 55: Your Guide to Fully Living the Rest of Your Life*. Here is part of what they said: "We name the periods of stability and the transitions by highlighting one feature characteristic of each" (16).

Extended Middle Age. We call the first period of stability "Extended Middle Age." This period begins when aging is acknowledged publicly, usually by Medicare eligibility. It is often difficult to observe any substantive changes in lifestyle from middle age. Typically, the beginning of this period coincides with the end of a career and may be referred to as retirement. People in this period are engaged in lifestyles difficult to distinguish from the lifestyles of 40- and 50-somethings. For some, what will be different is the absence of the rewards and demands of structured work environment; for others, there will be more of a redirection of effort than retirement from effort. For both, a difference may be the absence of children in the home. (19)

The period of Extended Middle Age is marked by a continuing sense of control alongside intimation of frailty, and it can last a long time. (20)

Ready or Not. Extended Middle Age most often ends in a transition we call "Ready or Not." The hallmark of this transition is loss, specifically loss that requires a significant change of lifestyle and a redefinition of your self in the light of changed circumstances. Such losses are most typically the death of a spouse, a one-sided divorce, or the deterioration of your own physical well-being or the physical or cognitive well-being of your spouse or partner. This transition may be required at any age, although the further one gets past 75 the higher the probability it will happen soon. (21)

The New Me. The Ready or Not stage is followed by the second stable period. We call this "The New Me." Most people in this period are still independent and in control of their own lives.

Whatever the new set of circumstances, and no matter how it constrains your freedom or how much it impacts your finances, you will need to embrace your new reality. Of necessity you will have to forge a new lifestyle, and a new life, around that reality. While you may be the same person inside, your circumstances have changed dramatically. For some, this period is difficult. For many, the adaptation to a new life is remarkably positive. For all, the process is uniquely individual. The new state of affairs can continue for years. In this stable period, then, one lives up to new tasks and opportunities. (24)

Like It or Not. The New Me ends in a personal passage into dependence we call "Like It or Not." No one likes it. (26)

What happens is this: you experience a growing inability to function independently. Either your body or your mind ceases to function adequately for you to get along in the world. Resistance to dependence is ultimately overwhelmed by the grinding reality of not being able to make it on your own. You need to be in an environment where you can get the help you need for daily living. (26)

This transition need not signal the death of the spirit or even of the capacity to be fully human, but the challenge here is to accept one's limits and to prepare to live in dependence with dignity. This transition is often traumatic; much of what you have prized all of your life slips away. This is where the habits of body and mind that define self, and of heart and soul that motivate relationship to others, will be tested. (27)

5

The Rest of Living. The Like It or Not stage ends in a third stable period we call "The Rest of Living." It is a potentially rich and engaged part of one's life, but it is also a time of dependence and frailty. From the vantage point of the middle years, it is the period of life most of us fear. Along with Like It or Not, this is the period most associated with "getting old" in daily conversation. (28)

The real challenge in this period—which can go on for many years—is to continue to express oneself and relate to others despite the limitations. There will be diminishments, but your humanity need not be diminished. (29)

Dying. The final transition we call, simply, "Dying"—but death is not simple. For virtually all of human history this transition has been seen as the culmination of life, as a religious event to be prepared for with one's whole heart and soul. (30)

But this is not the mood of our times. We live in a secular age, and even death is often removed from the religious domain. Nonetheless, for many, dying is life's last sacred act. Dying is more than just an end; it is a profoundly human event. Its quality is enormously important, and will have profound and lasting impact on the people who love you. (30)

With this model in mind, we now turn to a consideration of the kinds of pathways to personal and communal spiritual growth that persons in the last third of life might encounter in each of the stages we have just discussed.

Pathways to Spiritual Growth

In *Fashion Me a People*, Maria Harris identifies five ways in which a community of faith shapes or fashions a godly people: community, prayer, teaching, proclamation, and service. To her list, we add witness. We see these six pathways to personal and communal spiritual growth as key elements in the life of any community of faith. The importance of each of these pathways to spiritual growth is perhaps most easily seen if we try to imagine a church that lacks any one of them. It would not be a faithful or vibrant community of faith.

We believe that these six pathways to spiritual growth are of particular and specific importance in the lives of elders in the community of faith. When a church faithfully fashions those in the last third of life in these pathways, indeed there will be for these people—in the wonderful images of Kathleen Fischer—*autumn gospel* and *winter grace*.

We briefly describe each of the six pathways at this point. When we get to each stage of the last third of life, we will give substance and detail to ways in which each might take shape and be supported in a community of faith.

Community is based on a deep human need to belong, to be "not alone," to associate with those like ourselves, to be part of a group of common purpose. At its best, community responds to an immeasurable desire to be in a place of love, caring, and compassion. As Maria Harris notes, at a congregational level, community requires inclusion, leadership, and outreach. At a familial level it requires presence, receptivity, and responsibility.

Prayer is based on our belief in God's presence with us, our need to communicate with the Divine, and our awareness of our desire to entreat and our duty to praise. Its regular and rhythmic forms reflect our need for rituals, for order, for pattern. Prayer is both communal—where we are part of a worshiping community—and personal—where we spend our own time in the presence of God.

Teaching is a response to our thirst to know, to make sense of, to understand the universe and our place in it. Within the Christian community it refers to the "teaching of the apostles"—the teaching of those who were the first witnesses to the life, death, and resurrection of Jesus—the one whom God made to be Lord and Savior.

Teaching takes as many forms as there are ways of learning. It happens in many places; it uses speech and dance and music and play; it is preaching and prophecy; it is interactive and didactic. As a pathway to spiritual growth, it is the faithful attempt of the community of faith to put into words God's gracious presence.

Proclamation of the gospel is the preaching of the passion, death, and resurrection of the Christ. But as Maria Harris notes, the "good news" is a living and prophetic word. "My word . . . shall not return to me empty, but it shall accomplish that which I purpose, and succeed in the thing for which I sent it" (Isa 55:11). Proclamation promises a release from the social and economic forces that bind so many of our sisters and brothers in intractable poverty. Proclamation is the word of justice, compelling the community of faith to "let the oppressed go free" (Luke 4:18).

Service to others, or caring for others, takes place both within the community of faith and in outreach. Within the community of faith it ranges from church administration to making a place of worship accessible to all, from babysitting services to health promotion. In outreach, or what Maria Harris calls "social care," we try to make real and visible the Beatitudes: feeding the hungry, visiting those in prison, sheltering the homeless, clothing the naked. It extends from hands-on service to advocacy for sane and just public policies. Genuine service is always accompanied by reflection. It changes the caregiver and the recipient of care as we engage openly with those who, while materially less privileged than us, are our brothers and sisters in this world and the next.

Witness is rooted in the concept of martyrdom. From the stoning of Stephen to the present day, there are those who have lived and died for the faith. In communities of faith, there is a constant and persistent need for witness to the love of God. We learn by seeing as well as by hearing. Witness is, in this sense, a lifelong task that takes on urgency and focus in the last third of life, when the inevitability of death may put our values into sharp relief.

Lives and deaths can be witnesses to the love of God. They can witness to the need to leave behind those things we counted on for our self-esteem. They can witness to the need for a deliberate legacy of faith. They can witness to a conviction that experiences of love, trust, justice, grace, and forgiveness are of lasting value.

A Word to the Reader

This book has three audiences: (1) church leaders whose congregations include a large percentage of older adults, (2) those involved with continuing professional education events or persons preparing for ministry, and (3) older congregants themselves. We wish to address those who are in the last third of life because we are speaking about their lives, their spiritual journeys, their hearts and souls. They can be both learners and teachers.

In many ways this is really where the issues need to be worked out, not exclusively but substantially. Those of you who are further on into retirement need to share your experiences with those who are beginning. Those of you who have endured personal sickness or the death of a spouse can console and support those in that valley. Those who have grieved and gone on to build a new life alone can be compassionate and supportive of those just now taking these steps. Those who have endured the loss of independence in the basics of life can tell others, "It's survivable." Those who are dependent on others for daily care can share the ways you maintain your dignity and your openness to others. Those closer to death can show all of us what it means to die in the Lord.

This book is, then, about cultivating an informed conversation about some of the most important religious realities of life. Each chapter is tied to a stage of aging: Extended Middle Age, Ready or Not, The New Me, Like It or Not, The Rest of Living, and Dying. Each stage focuses on the six pathways to personal and communal spiritual growth: community, prayer, teaching, proclamation, service, and witness. (The order in which these occur in any chapter is not fixed.)

It is clear that all of us are called to prayer, for example, no matter at which of the six stages we find ourselves. It is equally clear that the way one prays and what one prays about change dramatically with the years. Prayer for one in Extended Middle Age is not the same for one who is in the Like It or Not transition. Or, how one witnesses in Dying is not the same as how or to whom one witnesses in The Rest of Living. Our readings and strategies reflect these diverse spiritual needs.

For each of the pathways, we present a short reading and a strategy for engaging the community of faith and those in the last third of life in reflection and conversation. The readings are chosen for their uniqueness, ability to speak to the issue, and excellence. They are introduced by brief reviews from the editors/authors of this volume and documented internally. The strategies range from retreats to rituals to service projects to sermons to Christian education events to new ways of praying to the lived testimony of faith and experience. Note: these are merely samples; we trust they will spark your pastoral imagination.

To you, our readers, we say welcome to a renewed reflection on the journey of life.

A Technical Note

A number of our sample strategies are suggestions for sermons. You will notice that we identify for each sermon a "focus" and a "function." We take these terms from Thomas G. Long's book, *The Witness of Preaching*. We have found them helpful in presenting our sermon suggestions in consistent form. As Long uses the terms, "a focus statement" is a concise description of the central, controlling, and unifying theme of the sermon. In short, this is what the whole sermon will be "about." "A function statement is a description of what the preacher hopes the sermons will create or cause to happen for the hearers. Sermons make demands on the hearers, which is another way of saying that they provoke change in the hearers (even if the change is deepening something that is already present). The function statement names the hoped-for change" (86).

Long states that the focus and function statements should fulfill three principles: they should grow directly out of the exegesis of the biblical text; they should be related to each other; and they should be clear, unified, and relatively simple.

One can prepare a sermon without using focus and function statements, of course, but we found them helpful. "Focus and function statements are merely compass settings for the sermon journey. They guide the preacher in the creation of sermons that possess unity, clarity, and a firm connection to the biblical text" (86).

Source Notes

James C. Fisher, "A Framework for Describing Developmental Change Among Older Adults," *Adult Education Quarterly* (Winter 1993) 76-89.

Maria Harris, *Fashion Me a People* (Louisville KY: Westminster/John Knox, 1989) 75-87.

Thomas G. Long, *The Witness of Preaching* (Louisville KY: Westminster/John Knox Press, 1989) 89-91.

Henry C. Simmons and E. Craig MacBean, *Thriving After 55: Your Guide to Fully Living the Rest of Your Life* (Richmond VA: PrimePress, 2000). Copyright © 2000. All rights reserved. Reprinted with permission of PrimeDynamics, LLC, P. O. Box 9797, Richmond VA 23228, 1-804/935-6800.

chapter 1

EXTENDED MIDDLE AGE

Witness: A Pathway to Spiritual Growth

READING

It was not until the late 1960s that "middle age" was identified as a separate part of the life cycle. Bernice Neugarten and Nancy Datan studied this phenomenon intensely, assessing in a variety of dimensions what was the subjective experience of middle age for the people they questioned. In this article, Simmons uses their categories and insights as a jumping-off point for an inquiry into group values then and group values now.

Given the increasing diversity of individuals as they age, how shall we describe a group [now in Extended Middle Age] in a way that has both precision and general applicability? In 1974, Neugarten and Datan described the "middle years" in a groundbreaking article. At one level this article is hopelessly outdated—middle age in 1974 is not the same as middle age in 1994. Yet the people who are now 63 were 43 when the article was written; those now 68 were 48, and so on. I find it very instructive to see what these travelers in time have brought forward in their caravan. In the section of the article titled, "The Subjective Experience of Middle Age," the authors deal with the subjective experience of age under several headings that are relevant in the lives of those in Extended Middle Age today: the delineation of middle age, distance from the young, marriage and family, the work career, the changing body, the changing time perspective, and the prime of life. (17)

The Delineation of Middle Age. It is clear in interaction with this group that there is a strong resistance to being identified as "old" and even to associating with those who are old. Certainly, there is for most a clear understanding that they are not middle-aged in the same way as they were at 43 or 48; yet they still know themselves (realistically, I would say) to be in "the middle years." Faced with the absence of a vocabulary to describe this time of life (Extended Middle Age is not common parlance), faced with the clear social stigma attached to being old, and faced with the need to resist giving in to the burdens of time, these people will continue to use situational rather than chronological clues to describe themselves. (19)

Yet positions within different life contexts are subtly or not so subtly shifting during this period. Even if the body is strong, it is—as it has always been—a treacherous indicator of the humanness of the person. There is a need to begin to transcend the body's strengths and limitations, at the same time as there is a need to be attentive to exercise, diet, and the physical joys of general vitality and everyday pleasures. There is a need to face with compassion in their bodiliness those who are now old. (19)

Distance from the Young. In their middle years this cohort reported themselves as the bridge between the generations and as having a clear sense of differentiation from both the younger and older generations. (21)

In late middle age at least 3 important shifts occur: (1) These people now stand between the old and those who are middle-aged, rather than between old and young. (2) Their cohort is more sharply defined, and both boundaries are more dangerous. (3) Issues become much more gender specific. Writing about women's perceptions of this time of life, Sarah Pearlman quotes a greeting card: "There comes an age in everyone's life when you have to stand up straight and tall, look yourself straight in the mirror and say . . . What the hell happened here?" (21)

Marriage and Family. In their middle years both men and women of this cohort "recognized a difference in the marriage relationship that follows upon the departure of children, some describing it in positive, others in negative terms, but all recognizing new marital adjustments to be made." There are several marital adjustments that need to be made (or better, negotiated) in extended or late middle age. At the beginning there is the adjustment of substantially more time together. (The old joke has a woman saying of her newly retired husband, "I married him for better or worse, but not for lunch.") Later there may well be the adjustment required by a beginning of diminishment of health for one of the partners. (21)

Other familiar roles may be necessary, namely as son or daughter. In this time of life there is often the need to deal with the prolonged frailty or death of one's parents. For some this is a (more or less) arduous human task. Frailty takes many forms, some of them enormously difficult to bear either because of physical and mental deficiencies or because, in old age, truths about relationships are revealed that cause profound disturbances and even alienation between old parents and late middle-aged children. Extended Middle Age may be delineated by such issues so that a period of years is absorbed in parent-care. (21-22)

The Work Career. There are educational tasks here for both men and women: (1) the appropriation of the cessation of full-time paid employment with the concomitant change in status and even self-worth, (2) the use of time that had been previously assigned to work and career, and (3) the transition from the world of work to the world of leisure. This latter task is particularly difficult for some for whom work has been so consuming that they can be described as "leisure incompetent." (22)

The Changing Body. In their middle years men reported that the most dramatic cues were biological. "Change in health and sexual performance are more of an age marker for men than for women." Women's concerns are vitally connected to those of their husbands. "Women are more concerned over the body monitoring of their husbands than of themselves. That widowhood is a critical concern for middle-aged women is born out by other studies." (24)

If these were the concerns of this cohort in their middle years, one may surmise that the concern is even more intense in late middle age. (There will be variations, of course, as not all women are married.) (24)

The Changing Time Perspective. In middle age the task was to be aware of the inevitability of one's own death and to begin to come to terms with that actuality. This may still be the task. It may be that this issue is closely bound up with the sense of "being in control" in the prime of life. (24)

The Prime of Life. There is a world of assumptions about the "perfectibility" of the human situation of a cohort that came through the Depression and successfully fought World War II. "These people feel they effectively manipulate their social environments on the basis of prestige and expertise, and that they create many of their own rules and norms." These are the people who, when they were middle-aged, described themselves as "in command." (25)

For this group, even the vagaries of fate were, in their middle years, understood as being "manageable" if they were on the correct schedule. Inevitably, the erosion of the years will temper this judgment: once-unanticipated events become anticipated traumas. I doubt, however, that the shift is easily made; control need not give way gracefully to an inevitable loss of control. (25)

SMALL GROUP DISCUSSION

PARTICIPANTS
   12 men and women in Extended Middle Age

FORMAT
   120 minutes, followed 2 weeks later by a 60-minute feedback session

OBJECTIVES
   • To describe the subjective experience of middle age for each sub-group of participants
   • To identify the values of each sub-group in regard to each of the 7 categories of inquiry (ex: work, career, family and marriage, distance from the young)

- To have the sub-groups identify how these same values would play out in today's world
- To have the participants select 1-2 of these values and decide how they will practice, and thus witness to, them

MATERIALS
- 4 sets of tables and chairs
- newsprint
- markers
- copies of Neugarten's/Datan's article

PREPARATION
Distribute copies of the Neugarten/Datan article to participants, inviting them to make notes or add comments.

INSTRUCTIONS
1. Divide the group into "birth cohorts"—in this case, those born in (or closest to) 1940, 1935, 1930, 1925. (5 minutes)
2. In table groups, have the participants discuss their subjective experiences of middle age (40–45) as they regard the 7 categories listed in the article. Ask someone from each group to record on newsprint highlights of his/her group's discussion, specifically, the following topics: What was their world like in regard to each category? What were the values specific to each category that were most typical of your group? (40 minutes)
3. Ask each recorder to report briefly to the group as a whole. Allow time for interaction between groups. (15 minutes)
4. In table groups, ask the participants to discuss how these values they discussed would be played out in today's world. What would the values look like? What would a person have to do to put them into practice? (25 minutes)
5. Return to the larger group and ask recorders to summarize their discussions. (15 minutes)
6. Ask participants to choose 1 or 2 values they are interested in taking as their own and to develop a specific plan for how these values will play out in action. Invite participants to share these with each other. (20 minutes)

7. After 2 weeks, reconvene the group. Ask each team to discuss among its members their experiences of putting their values into practice—that is, of witnessing. Then ask each team to explain to the larger group what their witness was, to whom they witnessed, and the strategy they used. Have each team give an assessment of their own work, highlighting strengths and weaknesses. Allow for dialogue and questions from other teams, with the caveat that the discussion be constructive and positive. Encourage the teams to continue their witness. Offer the possibility of reconvening the whole group at a determined later date. (60 minutes)

Prayer: A Pathway to Spiritual Growth

READING

Janice Brewi and Anne Brennan approach the spiritual perspectives of midlife from a broadly religious or spiritual point of view. In the excerpt that follows, they speak of ways to pray in language that is both Christian and Eastern. Indeed, some of their references (ex: to mantras and mandalas) may strike the reader as both unfamiliar and intriguing. For each of these terms, a brief definition is added in a parenthetical note.

At midlife each person needs to find what it is that brings him or her into the attitude of retreat and the expression and the language of prayer. Such retreats into prayer can last an instant, or an hour, or a month, or longer. To pray, one does not need God-language or words at all. The midlife person has had enough life experience to know this. In midlife one can be well beyond externalism. At this midlife stage people can look back and recognize true moments of prayer, whether they happened inside or outside the auspices of a particular religion or religious language. (117)

Before looking at some possible ways into prayer, one needs to look at what constitutes praying. Prayer is affirming God and oneself. Prayer is the whole person being attentive to God, longing for God, opening to God, reaching out to God, surrendering to God, needing God, centering oneself in God, communicating with God, offering oneself to God, resting in God. Prayer is the interiorizing of the Incarnation. Prayer is solitary and communal, personal and political. Prayer is profoundly immanent and profoundly transcendent; profoundly simple and profoundly mysterious. It is a knowing of God and a "not knowing." Prayer is a retreat with God in one's conscious ego, a regression with God into the unconscious depths of the self. There is no place where prayer is impossible. There is no time when prayer is impossible. There is no way in which every person must pray. (117)

Prayer is a whole-person activity; the body will be involved in this whole-person attentiveness to God. Thus, the body can help move the self into retreat and contemplation. One can, with the help of the body, create a center of peace within which the whole personality retires in God. (117)

The mouth has always been a part of the body that initiates a prayer state. One can voice the words of the psalmist or the written prayers of others, including all the scriptural prayers, to bring one's heart and mind to attend. Singing and chanting are ways to focus the self. Repetition of a mantra (a sacred verbal formula repeated in prayer or meditation) creates an atmosphere, reduces sense and emotional bombardments, and leads to repose. The mantra can be any simple phrase repeated rhythmically in harmony with one's breathing. Seven syllables are a help but not a necessity. (117-18)

The ears and the activity of hearing can bring one to the whole-person attentiveness of deep prayer. Listening to music, with or without words, whether it be designated as sacred or not, can be a vehicle for centering. Listening to falling rain, or to birds singing, or to children at play, or to the enthusiasm of young people, or to the sound of waves, a waterfall, or a brook, or to the spoken words of Scripture can lead one to prayer, and can be a form of deep prayer. Listening to the sounds in the silence can build a cathedral around a person in a dingy room. (119)

Seeing as well as hearing can be a way into prayer, which becomes prayer itself. Focusing on the light of a candle, or a meadow, or an ocean, or a mountain, or a beautifully shaped object, is looking with eyes that see. Watching a spider spinning a web, or ants building an anthill, or people in an airport can be praying. Going out to look at what tiny or great wonders are in one's own backyard, looking around at the colors and shapes and textures indoors or outdoors can engage the body, mind, and spirit in deep contemplation in the presence of the Lord of all. Gazing at a painting or a mandala (Hindu and Buddhist symbols represented by circular images) or a cross or a circle are ancient ways of presence. (119)

The whole body, in deliberate stillness or different motions, can lead one into prayer. Gestures, yoga postures, jogging, dancing, walking, sculpting are some possibilities. The great rituals and gestures of Christianity bring the whole body into an activity that is a retreat from "everydayness," and into a possibility filled with Presence. (119)

There is a whole-person involvement in the activity of writing a journal. One can create a dialogue on paper with the Lord or with someone out of the pages of scriptures or the lives of the saints that comes from the deepest center of one's self. One's prayer is written as one speaks to the other and writes the responses of the other. Writing about other aspects of one's inner life can likewise lead one to prayer. A spiritual journal is an ancient tradition. It is a memorial of inner dialogues and a way of capturing the Spirit. (119)

Prayerful reading of scripture involves the whole person, imagining oneself in a scriptural event and reflecting on all of the persons and their reactions. Being there in one's imagination can be a profound experience. The Scriptures are the verbalization of the religious experiences of thousands of people and paint a consistent portrait of their experiences of God. By reading scripture, one can learn to recognize the God experiences of one's own life. (120)

Focusing on one's breathing is an ancient and widespread way to prayer. The Hebrews saw breath as the breath of God. It is always a way of getting in touch with rhythm that produces profound effects. Focusing on the inner movements in one's body—the inner sensations and the outer sensations of touch—can make one present to oneself in a new way. Progressive relaxation of each part of the body has the same effect. Both can become in faith a kind of prayer to the God who incarnates Godself in each of God's images. (121)

PRAYER GROUP

PARTICIPANTS
people in Extended Middle Age

FORMAT
60-90 minutes

OBJECTIVES
• To introduce the participants to various ways of praying
• To allow the participants to explore various ways of praying

MATERIALS
• newsprint
• markers
• copies of Brewi's/Brennan's article

PREPARATION
Distribute copies of the Brewi/Brennan article to the participants.

INSTRUCTIONS
1. Begin with prayer. (5 minutes)
2. Using the material from the first section of the article, speak with participants about prayer at midlife. Summarize ideas on newsprint. (20 minutes)
3. Using the techniques suggested in "Focusing on One's Breathing," lead the participants in a time of prayer. (10 minutes)
4. At various times introduce the participants to other suggested ways of prayer (the mouth, the ears, seeing, the whole body, prayerful reading of Scripture). Allow them time to discuss and clarify what the authors suggest for each type. Provide whatever helps the authors have indicated as useful. Then, let the participants spend time practicing the particular way of prayer you are presenting. (20-25 minutes)

Teaching: A Pathway to Spiritual Growth

READING

*Rachel Dulin presents a phenomenological study of aging in the Hebrew
Scriptures, based on these major themes: length of days, physical and psychological characteristics of aging, the old in the community, and old age
as a time for human reflection. For the most part, the author has avoided
present-day interpretation of historical meanings.*

The Genesis writer may have had chronologies of heroes lost to us
yet important to him which he enumerated in order to attempt to
count the prehistorical data of the universe. Be that as it may, these
chronologies reflect the ancient writer's view of the lives of his prehistorical heroes. He admired them for their God-given gift of "length of
days."

Not one lost hearing or sight. Not one weakened, lost strength or
potency. They all remained youthful, vigorous, and productive. They
were bigger than life. They were true heroes. It was, indeed, a nostal-
gic view of the very distant past. (12)

It seems that the Genesis narratives were expressions of wishful
thoughts not to age with time, not to deteriorate as the years pass by,
not to suffer the pains of decrepitude. They presented a hope, projected
all the way to the far past, that although time would be counted, people would live long, but the aging dynamics would not be a part of their
experiences, and they, like their heroes, would remain ageless. (13)

Be it national or personal, the dream of "length of days" was an
expression of the denial of death and postponement of aging. It was
only a dream, a fantasy. The biblical writers of every era and social
strata were cognizant of the consequences of the passage of time.
Indeed, aging was very much a part of the social and theological reality of the ancient Israelite. (17)

The message of Psalm 71 is clear. The psalmist observed that in his
society people took advantage of the old, preyed on the aged and pur-
sued them to the end. God, on the other hand, was perceived as the
one who protected the defenseless, hovered over the weak, and "raises
him up from the depth of the earth" (Ps 71:20), the depth of

frustration, loneliness, and fear. [. . .] In turning to God for support the psalmist highlighted, in idealized terms, his expectations of others. He made it incumbent upon all persons to act with dignity, respect, and honor toward the aged. "Do not cast me off in old age" was not just a mere request from God but, rather, a demand upon all men and women to follow that course which is just and correct. (52-53)

The book of Ruth described the behavior of a family according to laws and customs which were known to its own society but which have become, in part, lost to us. It provides us with a glimpse of family interdependence where parents supported and cared for their children, and children, when their turn came, supported their parents. Just as the old nurtured and cared for the young, so the young were expected to support and provide for the old. From such a perspective, to be an aged member of a family meant to be protected by the family, to have a purpose in strengthening the family, and to be assured of a dignified life in old age. (62)

Was this a universal depiction of an ancient Israelite family? Probably not. This family's behavior stood in sharp contradistinction to the families of Samuel and Eli whose sons did not respect them or heed their words in old age (1 Sam 2:23-25; 8:2). It is quite possible that the plea of the psalmist who said, "Do not cast me off in the time of old age; do not forsake me when my strength is spent" (Ps 71:9), is in reaction to the fears and concerns of those elderly people in Israel who were not as fortunate as Naomi, and experienced loneliness, disappointments, and disrespect. (62)

The connection between old age and wisdom appears to be a natural one. Wisdom is a quality in human beings which is gained through life experiences. It is a process by which an individual behaves soundly and reasonably, basing his actions upon accumulated insights. The biblical text reflects an ambiguous view of the issue of wisdom and the process by which it is attained. At times such attainment closely reflects the experiences of the person in long life, yet, at other times, old age and wisdom are not correlated with length of days or multitude of experiences. (77)

As a matter of fact, much of the text describes the frustration of individuals who, in old age, could not distinguish between right and wrong (2 Sam 19:36; 1 Kgs 11:4). In doing so it reflects an opinion that wisdom is not necessarily the lot of the old, but, rather, a gift from God bestowed at any age and to whomever He chose. (70-71)

So we see that the biblical text portrays a society in which some were wise and some were fools, some were blessed with wisdom in young age and some gained it as time passed. Wisdom from this perspective was gained only through God's wish and regardless of the aging process. (77)

There were others in the biblical literature who looked upon aging as an holistic experience, an integral part of a person's life cycle. Writers like Qoheleth and the psalmist conceded that even though the aging process might not be gracefully experienced, nevertheless it could be a force to elevate the spirit and help find within oneself that spiritual component called the image of God (Ps 8:6-7; Eccles 8:1). (100)

There was no denial that old age had its limitations. Descriptions of physical decline echoed throughout the biblical literature. Yet old age brought with it a new dimension to human life; it ushered a new time. This was a time to think and a time to contemplate, a time to look at the world with renewed inquiring eyes and a time to appreciate God's creation. Through the realization of the finiteness of life there arose a renewed awareness of the beauty in it. (100)

And as for the condition of the elderly in society, laws were not legislated to protect the aged from societal ills, nor was society ever ready to listen to the prophetic voice which called for reform and change. However, human beings were given the ability and sensitivity to be inspired and to elevate themselves from despair, to create a condition of human life which is spiritually fed and meaningfully led. The physical blessings of old age—family, economic success, and health—were but a means to the attainment of the spiritual experience. It was through the spiritual experience that one exercised the freedom to trust in God and have unbreakable faith in Him. The biblical writers showed us that support during the aging years and in old age would not come from the outside, society at large but, rather, it would be found from within, in the human heart. (101)

The biblical writers viewed aging as a phase of life which affected individuals on a tri-dimensional level: personal, familial, and societal. The personal dimension was that by which each individual grew cognizant of the fact that life was short, that aging was the last phase of life, and that to age meant to face one's own mortality and vulnerability. The familial dimension of aging was that in which individuals faced responsibility for the protection and support of the aging members of their families: parents, grandparents, and other relatives. The younger members of the family were required to be attentive to the needs and provide the necessary care for the elderly members of the family unit. Lastly, the social dimension of aging was that which viewed the individual as part of the community, part of the whole. Each person's life intertwined not only with one's family but also with one's involvement in the community at large. (102-103)

SMALL GROUP DISCUSSION

PARTICIPANTS
> 10-12 people per intergenerational group (6th grade-adult)

FORMAT
> 90 minutes

OBJECTIVES
> • To learn about the images of aging in the Old Testament
> • To develop ideas that can change the image of older adults in participants' churches

MATERIALS
> • Bibles
> • newsprint
> • markers
> • copies of Dulin's article

PREPARATION
> Distribute copies of the Dulin article to the participants.

INSTRUCTIONS

1. Present a mini-lecture drawn from the Dulin article and from the following Scriptures: examples of heroes who were given "length of days" (Gen 23:1; 25:7; Deut 34:7; Judg 8:2); the notion of whether or not wisdom and respect come with age (Prov 16:31; Ps 92:14; Job 12:12-13; Ps 71:18; 1 Sam 2:22-25; 8:2-3); and the positive image we have of age in a familial setting (Ruth). Record Scriptures on newsprint to distribute to small groups. (10 minutes)

2. Form groups of 4-6 each. Instruct each group to discuss the way the biblical images presented in the mini-lecture are similar to or unlike the images we have in our society today of aging. Ask each group to appoint a spokesperson to report the group's discussion to the entire class. The spokesperson may choose to record the discussion on newsprint for later sharing. (20 minutes)

3. Assemble the small groups into a large group to hear reports from each spokesperson. Record the gist of each group's discussion on newsprint for the entire class to see. (15 minutes)

4. Have 'the small groups meet again. Instruct them to discuss what their church can do to make the image of older adults more positive within their congregation and in the community at large. (15 minutes.)

5. Reassemble the small groups into 1 large group. Ask each spokesperson to report to the large group any ideas generated by the small group. Record these ideas on newsprint to share later with the church board responsible for ministry within the church. (15 minutes)

6. A month or so after the information from the Bible study has been shared with the appropriate church board, communicate with the students that participated in the Bible study any changes in ministry that were generated from their ideas.

Community: A Pathway to Spiritual Growth

READING

Maxwell Jones, a social ecologist and psychiatrist, argues that social learning (including personal growth, old age, and mysticism) requires periodic exposure to a supportive and highly motivated peer group. With this support, "retirement" may become "freedom" to change, to set priorities based on contemplation, to question social stereotypes, to engage in social critique, and so on. The author addresses death, spirituality, contemplation, and the quest for truth.

Perhaps we should stop using the word "retirement" with all its negative connotations, and use instead the concept of "freedom." Freedom to read, to interact socially and to learn; freedom to change one's lifestyle and set priorities based on contemplation and absence of social pressures; freedom to question cultural stereotypes or the politics of fear and greed. Freedom to stand back and realize the growing loss of credibility afflicting the world of politics on local, national, or international levels and the lessening public confidence in medicine, law, economics, banking, and education. Freedom to explore absurd ideas, fantasies, and dreams that may in time come to reflect the limitations of our current concept of reality. (10-11)

In addition, we ourselves must change our own self-awareness, our understanding of who we are and why we are alive, instead of accepting passively the conformist attitudes, values, and beliefs of our success-oriented Western society. Can we, as older people freed, at least in part, from a conformist culture, make a significant contribution toward a world where understanding and compassion transcend the materialistic and technological outlook threatening our very existence? (13)

There is growing awareness among all age groups that everyone needs a support group. To segregate the age groups, the races, or the unwell and disabled is a phenomenon of our age and, except in special circumstances, is both unproductive and dehumanizing. The basic factor is that isolation engenders fear and paranoia, and throughout recorded history the tribal or social instinct in one form or another has been used to counter the vulnerability of the individual. In this age of social upheaval and fear of survival, the disintegration of our social lives calls for new patterns of social integration or support that reaches its height in old age. (14)

We seem to be at a crossroads in respect to reality. Our whole culture and education seek objective proof through our senses and the power of reason. The new reality bypasses objective proof and opens the way to an intuitive awareness of something vastly greater than self. By escaping from the bonds of a materialist, technological, scientific world, we seem to discover the secret of the universe, which includes everything known and unknown to man. To the Christian this means symbolically the Holy Trinity—Father, Son, and the Holy Spirit. Again we are intuitively aware of the energy and joyousness emanating from such an awareness, from the conversion of Saul to become St. Paul, to Martin Luther King's "dream." What a contrast to our ordinary lives when even the privileged university student tends to be drained of energy by the combination of an overloaded schedule, prescribed reading, and exams, leaving no time for contemplation and self-awareness. (66-67)

We tend to think of higher creativity or genius as something reserved for a few highly gifted people whom we can only admire or envy. There is a growing awareness that we may all have such latent potential, but that we reject the possibility without ever considering it seriously. It may be that the elderly in some instances, freed from the restraints of a routine job and caring less about appearances and the inhibitions imposed by our culture, are in a position to contemplate the meaning of life. If so, they may look inward and discover other more spiritual, intuitive, inspirational, or creative ideas. (103-104)

As is stressed throughout this book, we older people must set a standard for self-reflection, because we are in a favored position to do so. This is different from the concept of psychoanalysis which is concerned with the elimination of ego defenses or with repressed memories. Nor is it the long-term goal of selflessness, as attained through the discipline of meditation. By turning one's attention

inward and aspiring to achieve an open mind, allowing for contradic-
tory or paradoxical thoughts, and, freed from the lifelong pressures of
orthodoxy and educational conditioning, a new self may begin to
appear—a self that is akin to a subliminal consciousness. (106)

It is this self-awareness that has been largely lost in our Western
world, and that must be regained if we are to rediscover our lost
potential. Surely we must try to tune in to the impressions and feelings all around us that we tend to ignore; whereas, the shaman chooses
to talk to the trees, plants, and animals—and even to the rocks. This
self-awareness opens our minds to the wider field of intuition and to
our latent ability to get beyond the reality of the scientific rational
world in order to find a new reality in spiritual experiences, intuition,
and the mystery of life itself. We are still only vaguely aware of this
need to search for the truth if we are to escape from the illusion we
call reality. The need to find a deeper reality—which most of us have
only sensed momentarily if at all—is the major theme of this book
and, I believe, a major purpose of life. (106-107)

SMALL GROUP DISCUSSION

PARTICIPANTS

8-10 people who are at various stages of Extended Middle Age

FORMAT

90 minutes

OBJECTIVES

• To articulate thoughts, hopes, and dreams about the future
• To discern a new direction to take in participants' own lives

PREPARATION

Appoint several small group facilitators, preferably people who are
experienced in the dynamics of small group leadership. Have the
facilitators familiarize themselves with the guidelines for leading
the small group experience.

INSTRUCTIONS

1. Form groups of 4-5 people each. Have each group develop a covenant statement to which each member pledges to adhere. Cover such issues as terms of confidentiality and speaking only of personal experiences, therefore using only "I" statements. (10 minutes)

2. Ask the groups to discuss the topic, "new directions in my life." Some points of departure might be: "I have felt discontented with the way things have been going. . . ." "I don't know where to go since I stopped working. . . ." "I have dreams about where I want to be a year from now. . . ." "I have so many choices. How do I choose the right one?" (65 minutes)

3. When the groups have only 10 minutes left, the facilitators should help the participants come to some kind of closure (ex: agree to meet again or to explore personal options). (10 minutes)

4. Close with prayer, allowing time for the participants to pray aloud or in silence. (5 minutes)

Proclamation: A Pathway to Spiritual Growth

READING

David Maitland concentrates on issues central to a classical Christianity, as articulated in the Apostles' Creed. Specifically, he looks at the apostolic affirmations with an eye informed by the issues of midlife as these have been experienced in late 20th-century America. He does so on two assumptions: that any affirmation must be seen from some perspective—in this case his own life development—and that in relating such entities both may be made clearer.

By various evidences—the loss and/or graying of one's hair, diminished energy, slower recuperation from illness—it begins to become apparent that one is no longer young. Often accompanying these evidences is an increasing existential awareness of one's own mortality. That which we long knew intellectually—that someday we, too, would die—no longer seems as remote as formerly. This awareness of one's finitude is often furthered by the deaths of parents. Not only is this usually a grievous loss, but it catapults one into the unfamiliar role of being a family elder. Further, during the middle years one's children mature. No matter how much one has desired their increasing independence, one loses the privilege of being the parent of children who needed us more than they do in adolescence/early adulthood. Often this loss leaves parents uncertain about what it is that, in their unfamiliar freedom, they now want to do with their lives. As the result of years of living with deferred gratification—the needs of children often having taken priority over all else—such parents may not only not know what they really want, they may even be unsure that they have a right to do whatever they like. (7-8)

In addition to these unavoidable family-related losses, one often loses—either by death or by the mobility of society—old and trusted friends. (8)

Less discussable may be the loss of one's sense of invulnerability. Over the course of their lives most people experience either external caprice and/or their internal inadequacies. Couples who marry rarely anticipate the possibility of giving birth to retarded or handicapped children. Never are we prepared for the accident or illness which strikes down somebody close to us. From the outside and utterly beyond our control, we encounter life's unavoidable riskiness. I listened recently to some of the recordings of the English cellist, Jacqueline DuPré. Almost overnight her exceptional artistry was taken away by a progressively debilitating disease. Each of us knows comparable stories of people who took lifelong invulnerability for granted. (9)

It is one's attitudes towards many of life's basics—food, sex, work aspirations—which are subject to significant change in the middle years. Clearly, this is a time of life fraught with peril and potential. How one responds to these losses is both vital to future well-being and is the issue with which Christian faith must enable us to cope. We are dealing with the years in which, more clearly than most, our heart's restlessness is almost undeniable. That God may be our immediate trouble as well as our ultimate peace is precisely the issue which we may ultimately come to see. That is my thesis. (12)

The tasks of self-acquaintance in the middle years are not different in kind from those encountered earlier or later. However, at least
because of the number of unavoidable losses and their centrality to
one's matured self-understanding, the difference in degree from other
times of change almost amounts to a difference in kind. Even the ther-
apist knows the difficulty of working with intellectuals who tend to
assume that knowledge about something is all that is needed. Usually
such persons fail to recognize the crucial difference between the existential knowledge called for especially at midlife and knowledge which
may be adequate to the classroom. The task of the middle years is to
embrace as good and intrinsic to our present identity the cluster of
losses which we share with all persons, to admit kinship in frailty with
all humankind. At best we will be wounded healers, and our power to
heal will be in direct ratio with our ability to acknowledge our
wounds. (15)

Our role as Christians in these middle years is inherently difficult:
many want us to be towers of strength when we may be almost overwhelmed by our weaknesses. Further, we must overcome decades of
basically Greek thinking—in which we remained at a safe distance
from the objects known—because the thing to be known is no longer
"out there." It is now my losses which increasingly define me, my
aging which indicates that there is a new agenda to which I must
respond. It is no longer life's morning. It is at least the afternoon, and
we move toward evening. (16)

The struggle at midlife is that titanic—and that filled with potential for good. To be sustained in such effort, we will need a compelling
vision of God. Nothing less will enable us to resist societal powers
which urge conformity. (17)

So simple—and so elusive—until the experience of the middle
years may help us to recognize our sin as the refusal to be ourselves.
Much has been written about sin in quite different terms than these.
There is no necessary disagreement in differing statements. My point
is that sinful behavior always results from either over- or undervaluing
some aspect of God's creation. In this instance we have undervalued

those aspects of ourselves irrelevant to the pursuit of success. Sin follows. All the time that we were supposedly thinking about nobody but
ourselves, we have been busy thinking about anything but ourselves.
This is the legacy of the pursuit of success. This is why it is *spiritually*
lethal: it has caused us to act, and eventually to assume, that there was
nothing more to us than could be seen in our roles. Thank God for
the middle years in which we may discover by experience the inade-
quacy of the partial self which pretended that was all there was! (22)

By encountering a cluster of unavoidable losses, we may let go of
the pretense of self-reliance based upon a too limited self-acquaintance. This will not be easily accomplished; we have lived too long
within our limited selves. But, by God's grace—as in fruit which seeks
to ripen in the sunshine—there is that within us which desires
acknowledgment. There is the yearning for wholeness: "more of me"
wishes to be embraced, to be brought forth for the good yet to be
accomplished. However, unlike the ripening fruit, which will mature
as the sun shines, the inner yearning for shalom does not assure that
benediction. The struggle will be intense because there is a death
involved, and we do not readily die. It will be possible only as the
vision of God's unqualified love for us in our broken particularity
becomes more compelling than the vision which seemed to satisfy
during life's "morning." It will be possible only to the extent that we
can recognize the fraudulence of many of the assumptions by which
we have lived thus far. For complex reasons we will resist that recognition despite God's attempted tutelage at midlife, despite the
yearnings, until we are seized by the realization of the folly of our
efforts to justify ourselves. (22)

SERMON
TOPIC
    "Jesus looked at the person with love."

SCRIPTURE
    Mark 10:17-27, read with the Maitland article in mind

FOCUS

Because "with God all things are possible," whether or not we are able to respond now to God's call to redirection and change, Jesus still looks on us with love.

FUNCTION

To invite those who are beginning to distrust what they learned in life's "morning" to be the measures of success into a compelling vision of God's unqualified love for us in our broken particularity.

THEME

Jesus looked at the "rich young ruler" with love. Even when he was unable to "go, sell, give, come, follow," Jesus did not denounce him. Rather, he said, "With God all things are possible."

For all disciples, the spiritual meaning of this proclamation is that we must root out of our lives whatever may hinder our following Jesus. In midlife this means letting go of our sense of invulnerability, our built-up attitudes to many of life's basics, and our definitions of success. It means embracing our wounded kinship in frailty with all humankind, embracing our spiritual selves, being prepared to redirect our lives, and embracing a compelling vision of God's unqualified love for us in our broken particularity.

Whether or not we want it, we will have losses of things we previously held precious. These may be interpreted as God's loving invitation to us to "go, sell, give, come, follow," based not on our strength but on a God who looks on us with love.

Service: A Pathway to Spiritual Growth

READING

John Westerhoff and William Willimon, seminary teachers of worship and education (Episcopal and United Methodist, respectively), propose a ritual for retirement. It is composed of a declaration of purpose, a time of remembrance, a response by the retiring person, a blessing and sending forth. For this ritual to be effective, there should be a time of formal instruction beforehand.

People in our society are not proud to be old. Retirement often brings feelings of being "over the hill," of little use, incompetent, and without worth. (149)

These negative associations of retirement are especially troubling in a time when our country has an increasingly larger proportion of older people. What can the church do, liturgically and catechetically, to minister to people during the life crisis of aging and retirement? (149)

The goals of a liturgical response to retirement would be to help aging persons interpret this life passage in the light of the gospel, to prepare them for the challenges and opportunities of retirement, and to recognize these persons as persons of value and continuing importance whose lives and ministry are continuing rather than ending. Unfortunately, the closest thing we have to a ritual for retirement is the "retirement banquet" which is often a rather faltering, pitiful attempt to recognize this important milestone in a person's life; it usually makes the recipient of honor feel that he or she is being "put out to pasture" with a gold watch and a letter of thanks from the company president. For women who spend their working lives as housewives and mothers, we do not even have as feeble a response as a banquet and a gold watch. (149-50)

We must see aging and retirement not as a terminal phase in human development but as continuing the process of development. (150)

Any liturgical response to retirement must be part of a larger counseling and educational program for older people in the church. It must be a true rite of passage, designed to speak to the needed separations, transitions, and new incorporations which a retiring person must make. It may be done in a service of congregational worship, although it must be more than a new "old folks appreciation day." It may be a quiet ritual for the home or be a reception into a retired person's class or support group within the church. (150-51)

In a ritual for retirement, we could envisage the following parts (151):

- *Declaration* of the purpose of the rite; i.e., to recognize the retirement of someone from his or her job and to help begin a new life as a person who, now free from those demands and responsibilities, may begin a new ministry
- *Remembrance* of the job which is terminating; recollection, reminiscence, testimonials
- *Proclamation* through Scripture and homily of the beauty of a long and productive life, the joy of rest and recreation, the satisfaction of a job well done, an affirmation of our vocation as Christians rather than simply holders of a job, and encouragement for the fresh beginning which is now being made
- *Response* by the retiring person or family and friends to the proclamation
- *Blessing and Sending Forth*

One of the most significant, difficult, often unwanted and yet typically ignored passages in human life is retirement from the work force. Catechesis can help to prepare persons to understand the feelings that will accompany retirement and to consider the alternative life choices and lifestyles which are now possible. A catechesis of retirement needs to help persons understand vocation as spiritual pilgrimage instead of work, and ministry as the context for serving God and neighbors rather than employment. It can further help persons to understand the process of aging and the ongoing development of their spiritual life. (151)

Until this fundamental catechesis on retirement is done, it will be difficult to develop meaningful rituals for retirement. (151)

In preparation for retirement it is important that we aid all those affected by a retirement with attention to the family and mates of retirees. Everyone in a community needs to consider and prepare for the changes retirement will make in their lives. Even more important will be a catechesis that aids all involved to discern where God is now calling them and what new ministry they will need to prepare for. Catechesis for retirement could also rightfully prepare them for these new ministries. (150-52)

WORSHIP SERVICE

PARTICIPANTS

a congregation or long-term group with the church in which the retiree has been a member

FORMAT

a special service or incorporated into a regular service

OBJECTIVES

- To celebrate the transition to retirement
- To affirm the possibilities of new ministry that are available to the retiree

MATERIALS

- a token symbolic of retirement
- copies of Westerhoff's/Willimon's article

PREPARATION

Distribute copies of the Westerhoff/Willimon article to the participants.

INSTRUCTIONS

A few weeks before the worship service, ask for volunteers to work with the leaders on planning a closing ritual/worship service organized around the 5 steps proposed in the Westerhoff/Willimon article.

Source Notes

Bernice Neugarten and Nancy Datan, "The Middle Years," in *American Handbook of Psychiatry*, ed. Silvano Arieti, 2d ed. (New York: Basic Books, 1974) 592-608.

Henry C. Simmons, "Education in 'Extended Middle Age,'" in *Liberal Religious Education* 12, Spring 1994 (Boston MA: Liberal Religious Educators' Association) 15-27. Reprinted with permission of the publisher.

Janice Brewi and Anne Brennan, *Midlife: Psychological and Spiritual Perspectives* (New York: Crossroad, 1982) 117-21. Used by permission of authors.

Rachel Z. Dulin, *A Crown of Glory: A Biblical View of Aging* (New York: Paulist, 1988).

Maxwell Jones, *Growing Old—The Ultimate Freedom* (New York: Human Sciences Press, Inc., 1988)

David J. Maitland, *Looking Both Ways: A Theology for Midlife* (Atlanta: John Knox Press, 1985). Used by permission of author.

John H. Westerhoff III and William H. Willimon, *Liturgy and Leaning Through the Life Cycle* (New York: Seabury, 1980). Used by permission of HarperCollins Publishers.

chapter 2

READY OR NOT

❧❧❧

Witness: A Pathway for Spiritual Growth

READING

Joseph Sittler reflects on three things that have been on his mind since he was aware of the world: the nature of truth, the scriptural meaning of eternal life, and the nature of faith. This essay is the author's testimony about his enduring beliefs, including a conviction that the Christian story is most adequate to describe what he knows about human life.

All of this is by way of getting to the next theme which is something everyone wonders about, but few people talk about openly. What is the nature of eternal life? What does the term mean? (62)

The particular phrase itself, "eternal life," is a curious phrase. It is so illogical as to be absurd and improbable. The only possible meaning of life that we can certify and use as a kind of negotiable term which we can all understand is that life is characterized by temporality, mortality, passing-ness, mutability. Life comes, unfolds, closes, and departs. That is the only kind of life we know anything about. To use the adjective "eternal" about life is really to make no sense. Yet Jesus, who made sense, used the phrase. . . . What the Fourth Gospel calls "eternal life" . . . does not point to a life after death as its primary reference. It has little to do with resuscitation, a rerun of the life I've already had, or reenactment, repetition, or everlasting and endless

playback through all eternity. In fact, I would suggest that to understand the meaning of eternal life that way is not only not reverent, it
is positively blasphemous. It would be to raise egocentricity to an
absolute state: to want to be oneself for ever and ever, to regard being
Joe Sittler through all eternity, would be to raise the evil of idolatry to
an absolute pitch. Therefore the notion of eternal life, it seems to me,
is one which must be pondered. Can it possibly mean this—an
unfolding into a participation in that which certifies itself to you as
more than yourself, greater than yourself? Before, and during, and
after yourself, it *is*. It is participation in the depth of that Being which
underlies all being, a participation in the primal source of all that is.
It is active life in its temporality, qualified by eternity with such cele-
brative joy and vision as to deserve the phrase "eternal life." (62-63)

Faith is a kind of response to the allure, the allure that resides in
every living thing, every occasion. I do not reject the notion that some
kind of eternal residency with the Eternal is a hope of the Christian
tradition. But I cannot fill it with content. The New Testament does
not try to. "Eye hath not seen, nor ear heard, what God hath prepared
for those who love Him." It's interesting that St. Paul tried on one
occasion—two really, but one remarkably unsuccessful occasion—to
answer the question, "In what body shall the dead arise, and in what
form will they come?" . . . And then, after the end of his writing career,
in the Epistle to the Romans, he has one smart little sentence: "If we
live, we are the Lord's; if we die, we are the Lord's." Period. And that's
exactly what the New Testament says, and what the Christian faith
promises as a Christian hope: that is, if God is the Eternal One, and
if one be in Him in faith and participate in the Eternal, God does not
die. What does that mean for *me*? I don't *know*. But it could mean
nothing ill. (65)

The usual language for life after death is a language which I find
depressing: reenactment, eternal recapitulation, a living with one's
adorable selfhood for ever and ever. Don't you have any ambition?
Charles Hartshorne, the metaphysician formerly [. . .], said in an
essay called "The Abiding Present" that "in the mind of God we shall
never not have been." That is an interesting way to suggest what to me
is a way of pointing to the hope of eternal life. It's enough. (65)

SMALL GROUP DISCUSSION

PARTICIPANTS

youth and adults who are dealing with the death of a loved one

FORMAT

60 minutes

OBJECTIVES

- To identify some of the key questions of religion
- To understand that the language of religion is mythic not literal
- To apply this understanding to the death they have experienced

PREPARATION

1. Invite a youth, a middle adult, and an older adult to speak about the doubts, angers, and frustrations they still experience in regard to the death of a loved one.
2. Provide each participant with a copy of the Sittler article.

INSTRUCTIONS

1. Introduce participants to each other. (5 minutes)
2. Read aloud the final 2 paragraphs of the Sittler article. (5 minutes)
3. Invite the speakers to share their grief experiences. (15 minutes)
4. Ask all participants to reflect silently on these questions: Which of the points raised by Sittler make most sense to you? Where has the language of faith helped or not helped you deal with the death you have experienced? (3-5 minutes)
5. Ask participants to share their responses to the questions above. Emphasize that there are no right or wrong answers and that no one should respond to another's reflections. (10 minutes)
6. Ask the participants where they might be looking to Christian faith to solve the mystery of death, and where they are looking to religion to point to that place on the horizon beyond which is God. Help them see and claim the difference between these approaches, and apply this understanding to the death they have experienced. (15 minutes)
7. Read Romans 8:23-39 slowly and meditatively. (5 minutes)

Service: A Pathway for Spiritual Growth

READING

*James R. Adams' leader's guide for a study course on death and bereave-
ment notes that older people are, for the most part, willing to talk about
death. The course focuses on death and bereavement from a variety of
perspectives—biblical, societal, and practical.*

Many bereaved people have found what the church had to offer
them when the death occurred was of little help to them. That is not
to say they were disappointed; they probably did not expect much
help from the church. When you put yourself in the position of the
bereaved person, it is difficult to see how you could be helped by the
commonly accepted functions of the church. If your only problem
with the death is that your convictions about a future life are a little
uncertain, reassurance may seem to help a little. Actually, this kind of
assurance may be the church's way of saying what the rest of the
funeral practices indicate: the dead are not really dead, and no real loss
has taken place. This amounts to a denial that grief is appropriate.
Sometimes this point of view is pressed on the bereaved not only by
their clergyman but also by their friends, because neither the clergyman nor the friends can tolerate being around a person who is visibly
upset. Well-meaning people may also harbor the mistaken notion that
intense emotions are bad for anyone and should be curbed either by
drugs or by assurances that there is nothing to be upset about. (45)

Unfortunately, such assurance that the dead are at peace in heaven
can prevent a susceptible person from acknowledging grief—with the
consequence in later years that the repressed feelings of anguish
become emotionally, even physically, destructive. (46)

Church people are often of little help to you in your grief because,
like the rest of society, they tend to deny the awful reality of your loss
by talking to you about heaven. They also normally fail to recognize
the other sources of the pain you experience in grief, those that result
in what we have called the sting of death. The stabbing pangs of
regret, the choking heat of anger, and the nagging ache of genuine
doubt are as unacceptable to most church people as they are to the

world at large. Grief supposedly is the result of loss, and the solution is heaven. If the solution does not work, it is your fault for not believing firmly enough in life after death. What may be the primary source for the anguish experienced in bereavement is not recognized, nor in any way acknowledged by the church people. From what you hear in the comfort they offer, you are usually led to understand that you must not worry about what might have been in the past, you must above all convince yourself that the dead are at peace in heaven. Because of the penetrating reality of their own experience, or because of their basic honesty, many people are unable to follow these implied admonitions. For them the church is no help, and they know it. Perhaps the plight of those who think they are being helped is worse; they are being deceived and being taught deception by what the church people offer as their solution to the problems created by death. (47)

Death makes all human attempts at grandeur and wealth seem vain and foolish. Death is a reminder that "our misdeeds" and "our secret sins" cannot be hidden or forgotten. If we had no regret about the way we spent our lives, death would not hold the terror which it does. Pretending we have no regret may make death less awesome, but it requires of us that we forsake honesty and live a lie. (51)

In the face of death, sin is the pretense that death is not real and that a loss has not occurred. Sin is the hiding of our genuine responses to death, the refusal to recognize our regret, our anger, and our doubts. Death receives its power over us precisely to the extent to which we sidestep the reality of our loss and of our feelings. The agony of grief which weakens and destroys our will to live creatively is the result of our sidestepping. The permanent estrangement from God which leaves us comfortless is the result of sidestepping reality, for God is the depth of what is real. The sting of death, as we have already discovered, is indeed sin. The victory over the power of death belongs to those who have faced the reality of what has befallen them both within and without. (54)

Death is not subject to logical explanation because it is part of the awesome mystery of creation. When we attempt to alleviate its terror by the use of reason and analysis, we destroy the possibility of personal encounter with God because neither God nor God's creation can be reduced to a logical formula. (57)

In bereavement the "yes" to our existence and to the one who gave existence to us may be difficult to say. The "yes" is admitting that from our experience all we can see of life is a coming out of nothing and a going into nothing. Taken on the face of it, life is senseless, but in faith we do not invent meanings or purposes for our existence because these obscure reality and lead us away from God. The "yes" is also admitting that death terrifies us, robs us of those we love, and leaves us in anger, regret, and doubt. Faith is telling the truth to ourselves and discovering the power to live in the truth, unprotected by denial or illusion, and affirming the source of that power. (66)

GROUP DISCUSSION

PARTICIPANTS

8-20 congregants who are responsible for the care and support of others in the community of faith (ex: deacons, communion ministers, Stephens Ministers), particularly grief ministry

FORMAT

90 minutes

OBJECTIVES

- To experience how well-intentioned remarks can do harm to the recently bereaved
- To explain the importance of active listening
- To understand more fully participants' roles as compassionate companions to the bereaved

MATERIALS

- newsprint
- markers
- 2 women's hats
- 2 men's hats
- copies of Adams' article

PREPARATION

1. Distribute copies of the Adams article to participants.

2. Enlist 2 people to play the proper role of comforter in bereavement ministry (see Characters 2 and 4 below).
3. Display 4 pieces of newsprint in the classroom, with a hat attached to each.

INSTRUCTIONS

1. Form groups of at least 4 people each. (5 minutes)
2. Ask each group to create and name each of the following characters to go with each hat. (15 minutes)

- Character 1—a distraught woman whose husband of 12 years has died in a car accident, and who is filled with anger, regrets, and doubts
- Character 2—the "comforter" to Character 1 who goes on and on about how happy the husband must be in heaven with Jesus
- Character 3—a man whose wife of 28 years died of cancer recently, and who has lost the will to live creatively
- Character 4—the "comforter" to Character 3 who drops by to visit and "cheer him up" by reminding him what a wonderful home and job he still has and how he ought to get on with life

3. Reassemble the large group. Ask Characters 1 and 2 from each small group to play their assigned roles. (10 minutes)
4. Ask participants to describe how they felt and how they think each character felt. Gently point out where participants are themselves getting into a "Job's comforter" role. (15 minutes)
5. Ask Characters 3 and 4 to play their assigned roles. (10 minutes)
6. Ask participants to describe how they felt and how they think each character felt. Gently point out where participants are themselves getting into a "Job's comforter" role. (15 minutes)
7. Discuss active listening (hearing feelings; responding to feelings with attention, support, permission to say whatever is on the heart) and the need for silence and a healing touch. (5 minutes)
8. Ask the previously enlisted "comforters" to play the proper roles of Characters 2 and 4. (10 minutes)
9. Debrief to check on leftover feelings or confusions. Pray to be compassionate as God is compassionate. (5 minutes)

Proclamation: A Pathway for Spiritual Growth

READING

For Herbert T. O'Driscoll, nothing is outside the realm of spirituality, although many of the practices of the devout life only now are being appropriated by many Christians. He states: "I am convinced that those of us who will live out our senior years through the close of this century are the fortunate recipients of a rich inheritance of spirituality only recently recovered. To realize this can be a most valuable corrective when we are in a mood to lament the quality of our time in history" (2).

Human experience is unthinkable without its also being a spiritual experience from birth to death and beyond. In the life of any particular individual there may be no institutional form of spirituality, no church envelopes on the writing desk, no familiar hymns learned or creedal statements formed. But we are as much spiritual beings as we are sexual beings. To be human is to be spiritual. (2)

I shall age in the company of many spirits, welcome and unwelcome. Now halfway through my sixth decade, I sometimes detect the cloying presence of a spirit of self-pity, sometimes a spirit of fear, frequently a spirit of anxiety. All can at this stage be repulsed by activity, involvement, creativity, but I am under no illusion that these diversions will forever be available as allies against the invasion of those dark shadows of my being. Which spirit will be the richest and closest companion of my senior years? I do not yet know. I know what my hope is: that I may encounter one who offers new creation in exchange for my diminishing powers, bright visions for my failing sight, and intimations of resurrection for my expectations of death. (2)

Christians of all ages are discovering the flow of energy that comes from a faith stance that is consciously chosen rather than merely inherited and therefore sometimes taken for granted. They are coming to a deeper appreciation of the sacred meal of the Christian community that we call Eucharist. They are realizing the powerful way in which it can gather a people as they journey through a wilderness of change and threat. They are realizing that however fine and dignified our formal religion may have been, there may also have been an aspect of shallowness. There is in many a sense of moving into something deeper and richer. External things, things learned cerebrally, are yielding their single dominance to include more richly the internal, the experience, the intuited. We are recovering a sense of mind and heart informing us equally. Christian religion has rediscovered Christian spirituality. Religious system is enriched by spiritual journey. Faith is being more and more understood not merely as a body of knowledge we do or do not believe but also as a mystery which can give meaning to our experience and become a resource for our daily living. (5)

At the heart of all this, a revitalized liturgy proclaims the central and indispensable truth for this or for any other generation of Christians: "Christ has died; Christ has risen; Christ will come again." This short exclamation sings that human life is not merely a journeying away from a youthful innocent awareness of Christ as Lord and friend toward a sad and wiser adulthood beyond such naivete. We possess a Christ who is the resource for this hour and for all that lies ahead. He is Lord of the past, the present, and the future. Our years are a lifelong pilgrimage toward the Lord. (5)

Much more follows from that realization. The central events of Christian faith take place not only in the past but within the ongoing experience of our daily lives. Bethlehem and Calvary and the Garden Tomb are not merely places in a long-ago time or a faraway geography. Daily within each of us something of God seeks to come to birth. Each of us is potentially a Bethlehem. When I wrong or betray or hurt others, there is a sense in which I crucify them. In like fashion, I am myself subjected to little crucifixions. In such ways each of us can become a Calvary. But then the mystery we know as resurrection can also take place within each of us. We can recover from crushing defeat. We can transform destructive attitudes. Faith can overcome doubt, despair give way to joy. In such experiences we possess in ourselves the transforming power of resurrection. (6)

One other element of contemporary spirituality must be named. For a long time the Christian message was focused on personal life, its relevance seen primarily in terms of the individual. Still, there have always been those who challenged such a limited vision. Old

Testament prophets inveighed against it in their day, John Wesley and Elizabeth Fry in theirs. We have heard Dorothy Day, Thomas Merton, Martin Luther King Jr., Dietrich Bonhoeffer. These men and women, and many others, would claim that Christ is Lord not only of personal life, but also Lord and Judge of institutions—corporate, political, and, for that matter, ecclesiastical. (7)

SERMON
Topic
   "The Glory of the Lord at Each Stage of the Journey"

Scripture
   Exodus 40:34-38, read with the O'Driscoll article in mind

Focus
   Because God is intensely present with God's people at each stage of the journey, we can embrace the journey of aging—even when it means the losses of this stage—as a place of God's glory.

Function
   To invite those who undergo these losses (and those who stand with them) to see the fire and cloud of this part of the journey of age as revealing the glory of God.

Theme
   God's people do not travel alone. At each stage of the journey the central events of the story of salvation take place in the ongoing experience of our daily lives. In the bright daylight of the last third of life the glory of the Lord invites us to a more attentive spiritual journey. Even in the darkness of this transition, the presence of God can burn like a fire that consumes anxiety, self-pity, and fear. As a congregation, we need to stand with those who endure these losses. To those of you who are at this part of the journey, put your trust in God. Let God's consuming fire consume the anxiety that keeps you from asking for help, the self-pity that masks the heroism demanded, and the fear of a future that looks bleak.

Teaching: A Pathway for Spiritual Growth

READING

This selection by Henry Simmons was occasioned by a conversation with two colleagues, a Muslim and a Jew, about what—if anything—our traditions have to say to people with Alzheimer's disease or other dementias.

This is the "vision thing." What do we see, believe, expect is the goal of human life, the final measure of the human? To what are we called? What is written into the structure of human life that tells us about the nature of the last years? In religious language, what is God's will for old age? (4)

There are two enormously different, diametrically opposed, and competing visions. The first sees the end of human life as decline and failure. This is the prevailing view of mass American culture, which adores youth. Old age as failure, in Darwin's term as retrogression or backward development, needs no elaboration. (4)

The other vision—less compelling, perhaps, but more true to the spiritual traditions—can be pieced together from several sources: Hindu, Buddhist, Christian. For Hindus and Buddhists, enlightenment is the goal and end of human life. For Christians, one articulation of the goal or end of human life is eternal light. All die into the light. The Christian tradition might seem to focus entirely on life (or light) after death, but there are at least two reasons to rethink this approach. First is a weakening of any sureness about continued personal, individual existence after death. This is not only cultural; at least some Christians find a certain *hubris* in claiming that we will go on and on as very twentieth-century Western individuals after death. Others suggest that being in God in some more cosmic sense respects the tradition without distracting from the once-for-all nature of this life. (4)

The other reason to rethink this approach (eternal light as the goal of a life to come) is made clear in a controversy in the early years of this century in Roman circles. The question was asked whether all Christians are by their baptism called to mystical union with God in this life or whether this was for the chosen few. (The context of this question was whether, in the seminary curriculum, ascetical and mystical theology should be part of moral theology [religious ethics] or whether they should be treated separately.) The opinion of Père Garrigou-Lagrange prevailed, namely, that all are called to mystical union in this life. Enlightenment, mystical union . . . or failure, retrogression. This is the "vision thing." To which vision we respond is of critical importance for understanding spirituality in old age. (4)

I also wish to inquire about what is the phenomenon of very old age—what do we see and observe, what do the old report. Let me gather my remarks into two parts: physical frailty and mental frailty. (4)

For most in old age there is a time when sight, hearing, taste, smell grow dim or dark. Most people lose some acuity of sight (the world of visual beauty); taste and smell grow less sharp; the world of sound— voice, music, and noise—becomes less distinct. This darkening of the senses is a physical metaphor for a more general frailty experienced by most in old age. (4)

Metaphorically we might call this [mental frailty] a darkening of the spirit—also happens in two quite different ways: socially, many find themselves put aside—cast out into the darkness of social isolation. The old are relegated to live with the old or as the old, under the shadow of a collective cultural judgment that oldness is of no worth. Physically, for some there is a darkening of the mind. (4)

This brings us then to the spiritual traditions. In Buddhism and Hinduism there is a literature that speaks of an enlightenment that happens during life. In East and West there are fairy tales and folk wisdom that speak of self-transcendence in the old. In Western Christianity there is a common wisdom that in the spiritual life purgation precedes illumination and union. There is also a literature of mysticism that speaks of the dark night of the senses and the dark night of the soul: the first a purgation for the spiritually immature, the latter a step towards union. (5)

From these four strands we may begin to fashion a possible spirituality of old age that offers promise and is connected to the wisdom of a powerful (if neglected) part of the spiritual traditions. (11)

GROUP DISCUSSION

PARTICIPANTS

> 8-20
>
> a mixed group of recent retirees, people who are close to failing health, and people who are in frail health, or a group of church members or a combination of nursing home residents and volunteers who have recently retired

FORMAT

> 60 minutes

OBJECTIVES

> • For older, frail adults to share what their spiritual life has been like
> • For younger older adults to gain insight into the aging process and to better equip them to be volunteers with their elders
> • For older adults at various stages to explore God's role in the aging process

MATERIALS

> • newsprint
> • markers
> • recordings of quiet music or chants/sounds
> • copies of Simmons' article

PREPARATION

> 1. Distribute copies of the Simmons article to participants.
> 2. Arrange the classroom with comfortable seating; provide incandescent lighting.

INSTRUCTIONS

> 1. With quiet music or sounds/chants playing, ask the participants to sit in silence, relaxed and with their eyes closed. Ask them to envision what their lives will be like in 5 years. In particular, have them focus on what they envision their relationship with God might be like. (10 minutes)
> 2. Form small groups of 4-5 each, with both younger and older senior adults represented. Ask each group to choose a recorder/secretary. Have group members share the visions they had

during the period of silent reflection/meditation. Encourage
the groups to discuss the visions that are shared. (15 minutes)

3. Reassemble the large group. Ask the recorders to report on the
   visions shared in their groups. Allow questions during this time,
   but emphasize that no one is required to answer. (10 minutes)

4. Ask the large group to return to their small groups and there to
   discuss any physical and/or mental frailty that was a part of the
   vision each member had. If there are older, frail adults in the
   small groups, invite them to share their experiences with physical and/or mental frailties. Ask the groups to consider where
   God is in the visions they have had. (10 minutes)

5. Reassemble the large group. Ask recorders to give synopses of
   the discussions in their groups. Engage the large group in a discussion of where the darkness is and where the light is in the
   images that have been shared. Again ask the question of where
   God is in all this. (10 minutes)

6. Close with prayer that invites God into both the darkness and
   the light of our lives. (5 minutes)

Prayer: A Pathway for Spiritual Growth

READING

*"The second half of a woman's life offers some of the most complex and
spiritually rich decades she will know. We are only beginning to fully recognize their challenge and promise" (1). Kathleen Fischer explores the
decades of the middle and later years by weaving together stories, experiences, and research from a variety of traditions and cultures related to
aging and spirituality.*

Women have never lived as long as we are living today. That
means there are no established maps for the divine epiphanies we
might encounter. In the middle and later decades we meet God in new
ways. There are the agonizing losses and the unexpected graces, the
things we thought we knew about God that disappear as life moves
on, and the unfamiliar faces of the holy that appear in surprising
places. There may be long periods when the God of our childhood

disappears, leaving a vacancy that is not filled by any other belief. We become more aware of the depth and range of evil in the world, and try to reconcile our images of God with this consciousness. It is possible for our relationship with the Divine to become an adventure filled with fresh revelations. (74)

God appeared to the Israelites wandering in the desert both in the darkness of the pillar of cloud and in the brightness of the pillar of fire. Our own path to the sacred may also be one of darkness, absence, and not knowing. Darkness is a dimension of all contemplation. For some, this darkness comes and goes; for others, it is the persistent path. In both instances, it can become a fruitful kind of darkness. Women describe the context and quality of such darkness in numerous ways:

It is as if there were a table in the room with a gift on it, but I can't see it. My faith used to sustain me, but God feels distant now. I believe He is there, but I can't feel anything.

I fear being led into that darkness again, but I know it has been a rich place for me before. I have a strong sense that God *is*, but I can say nothing *about* God. My prayer is empty, and yet I am drawn to it. My God is now a dark God.

It is as though there is a black hole, a great emptiness, at my center. It feels like a lake drained of water; or as if an ice cream scoop had scooped out all there is, down to the bottom.

Though darkness and emptiness in prayer can be sustaining experiences, it is important to recognize that for many women the sense of God's absence is painful and puzzling. We wonder if there is something the matter with us. We are angry at God or at the darkness. We fear it will never end. We feel guilty, and search to see what we have done to deserve this darkness. This is especially true if the darkness is a loss of a former way of knowing God. For example, a woman remembers how in her earlier years she rejoiced in God's felt presence and had it with her all the time. Then it was gone. She yearned for its return. She was frightened and felt she had lost her way. There seemed to be no one there to help; even the God on whom she had once relied was gone. (79-80)

The notion of impasse is helpful because it does not minimize the suffering and frustration that can accompany spiritual darkness and emptiness. Yet it suggests that an impasse can be a condition for growth and transformation—if we face our sorrow and powerlessness; if we can identify and express our anguish; if we can relinquish our demands for clarity and actively surrender our need for control. It is difficult to do this alone. That is why a spiritual guide or friend is especially important at such times. (80)

It is possible, on one level, to distinguish spiritual darkness from the darkness of depression and grief. Spiritual darkness is often accompanied by several signs: peace at a level deeper than the surface agitation and distress, a desire for spiritual experiences and a longing to pursue them even though usual forms no longer give satisfaction, and good functioning in the other areas of one's life. In other words, if we are maintaining work and relationships and wish to stay with this dry knowledge and awareness of God that does not satisfy the senses, then the combination of these three signs indicates life and growth. Such darkness in prayer does not incapacitate us. (81)

Yet because of the interdependence of body, mind, and spirit, such distinctions are not so easily made in actual life. Some forms of darkness stand out in bold relief as either paths of prayer or periods of depression. At other times, the kinds of darkness intertwine. Our relationship with God is part of all life experience, and intersects with it. Depression and grief frequently blanket our prayer and our experience of God. At such times we know spiritual, as well as emotional and physical, darkness. Feelings of fear and sadness at times accompany loss of the felt experience of God's presence. We may mourn this absence or struggle with depression because of it. The magnitude of the changes we experience, and their impact on the rest of our lives, rather than the ability to distinguish one kind of darkness from another, may be what determines the kind of support we need. In the end, the same spiritual challenges exist in all kinds of darkness: to know that God is somehow present even when this is not apparent, to see the impasse as a call to new hope and vision, to find in the dying the paradoxical opportunities for life. (82)

Prayers that speak the language of the body are especially powerful when words alone no longer suffice. (93)

GROUP DISCUSSION

Topic
    Kinetic Prayer

Participants
    a women's group

Format
    60-90 minutes

Objectives
- To provide the participants with the opportunity to experience prayer using their bodies rather than their thoughts or words
- To allow participants to find a spiritual friend with whom they may continue practicing kinetic prayer

Materials
- religious art
- recorded religious music
- a cross
- candles
- copies of Fischer's article

Preparation
1. Distribute copies of the Fischer article to participants.
2. Set up a meeting area for the large group using comfortable seating, incandescent lighting, and aromatic candles.
3. Set up various places for experiential prayer. Suggestions:

- Develop a labyrinth in the sanctuary by establishing a path to weave among the pews.
- Construct a labyrinth outdoors or in any large room.
- Display religious art (i.e., a painting, an icon, a tapestry, a sculpture) in a room.
- Have a variety of recorded religious music playing in a room (ex: chants, organ, choral, instrumental).
- Place a cross in the center of a room, and arrange candles around the cross.

INSTRUCTIONS

1. Have a time of introductions.
2. Explain that the participants will have the opportunity to experience praying with their bodies rather than words and thoughts. This will be a sensory experience using their sight, touch, smell, hearing, and movement. They should allow themselves to be open to God's presence in whatever form it takes. Emphasize that all these prayer journeys are to be done in silence. Explain the following choices for kinetic prayer:

- The center of the sanctuary labyrinth may be the chancel area where the participants stop their movement for a time before weaving their way out of the labyrinth.
- Using the senses of touch and sight, the participants may pray using art as a focal point.
- The participants may listen to recorded religious music and move their bodies with the music in the form of prayer.
- Ask participants to depict with their bodies their prayers to God. For example, thanksgiving and jubilation for God's goodness can be expressed by raising their arms and gazing upward. They could rock back and forth to express grief. Ask participants to be creative as they search for ways to express their prayer without using words.

3. Ask if there are any questions or apprehensions about the kinetic prayer experience. Invite participants to choose those they would like to experience.
4. Reassemble the participants to discuss their prayer experiences. Emphasize that sharing of their experiences is voluntary. Propose to the participants the idea of finding a spiritual friend in the group with whom they may continue praying in any manner they choose.

Community: A Pathway for Spiritual Growth

READING

Paul Maves completed his doctoral dissertation on the church, the community, and the "aged" in 1949. For the next four decades he wrote and taught about the place of the elderly in the life of the church. The way in which he framed the issues in this 1954 article may seem dated, but the direction and impetus in his work are still fresh and compelling, and the challenge he poses has not fully been taken up by communities of faith.

Without a reason for living, health is useless and soon breaks down. Without a reason for living that integrates a person with society, psychological conflicts arise. (11)

First, religion attempts to come to terms with ultimate reality and to discover meaning in life. It represents the search for ultimate values. It holds that persons are of more value than property, that love is better than hate, that man [sic] is an end in himself [sic] and not a means, that the individual is the end and the institution the means. It is religious faith, not science, which affirms that the geriatrician's quest is worthwhile. (12)

Second, in the attempt to come to terms with reality, religion faces the limitations of life and attempts to find meaning in disease, disability, delinquency, and death. It acknowledges finiteness and seeks to enable persons to live with mystery through faith. (12)

Third, religion provides a channel for the expression of our gratitude for life's innumerable blessings, and enables us to celebrate our joys and our triumphs with all the artistic skill at our command, recognizing that many of these gifts come unsought and unearned. Among these gifts are the gifts of life and love. (12)

Finally, religion binds men [sic] together in a common commitment to values which it then attempts to make operative in human life. Inevitably a religious view of life gives rise to a fellowship, and this fellowship becomes structuralized in an institution with its creedal statements, ceremonies, and patterns of conduct which express the values to which it is committed. Religion not only gives life meaning but also makes society possible. (12)

Religious faith says that a man [sic] is of intrinsic worth in himself because he [sic] is a child of God, and finds that one can be creative in terms of human values even when he [sic] can no longer be productive in economic values. (13)

With this analysis of the function of religion we can now outline the role of the church in relation to community planning. To begin with, the church has a goal-setting and value-setting function which may give impetus, purpose, and direction to community planning. This may operate indirectly as the members of the church bring their ethical ideals into their responsibilities as citizens. It may work directly as the church takes the lead, perhaps with the counsel of such experts as geriatricians, in evaluating community patterns and resources in their effect upon older people and in suggesting desirable goals. (13)

In the second place it may take the initiative in stimulating community planning in order to implement the goals and values it cherishes, so that community relations will not be in conflict with the quality of the relations which exist within the inner community of the church. (13)

Thirdly, the church may cooperate with other agencies in securing the necessary resources which older people may need to handle their conflict creatively, to resolve their tensions successfully, to achieve satisfactions adequately, and to find support and security. Such agencies include counseling centers, referral agencies, hospitals, homes, recreational facilities, and home care services. Church groups may also study housing and social security with a view to their responsibility. (13)

SERMON

TOPIC
"Armchair Quarterbacks Need Not Apply"

SCRIPTURE
Matthew 22:34-46, read in light of Maves' article

FOCUS
In this discourse Jesus is explaining to the Pharisees that the basis of our relationship with God—love, which we freely receive from

God—requires an active response to love God above all else and to love our neighbors as we love ourselves. The reality to which this might refer is the awareness of the congregation that some of its members are undergoing the losses of the Ready or Not transition.

FUNCTION

To invite us to consider ways that the church can become involved with what Maves calls "community planning for the aged."

THEME

If we are to love God with all our hearts, souls, and minds, and love our neighbors as we love ourselves, we are called to do something. We all know that if a congregation is to pursue a course of action, the congregation as a whole needs to support it. The activity also needs to be chosen with the strengths of the congregation in mind so that the love of neighbor may be fulfilled.

When viewed in the broader context of Matthew's Gospel, Jesus' exchange with the Pharisees in Matthew 22:34-40 is the final of 4 questions the Pharisees or Sadducees have put before Jesus. He has bested them in each question and has amazed them with his answers. They have hoped to be able to trip him and show that he is a heretic, but each of his answers has been orthodox. Jesus turns the tables and asks the Pharisees a question. They, too, give an orthodox answer, but show that they lack the faith to understand how the Messiah can be the son of David and David's Lord. Jesus points to the Pharisees as having knowledge to impart, yet failing to practice what they teach. On the other hand, Jesus' entire life demonstrates how to fulfill the greatest commandment.

We are called to action if we are to love our neighbor as ourselves. With Jesus as a model, each congregation should be involved in its community in ways that demonstrate God's love for each person. The best way to be involved in the wider community is for a church to plan an outreach based on its strengths. For example, a church may choose to be involved in ministries at counseling centers, referral agencies, hospitals, homes, recreational facilities, and home care services.

Source Notes

"The Last Lecture: A Walk Around Truth, Eternal Life, Faith," by Joseph Sittler, is reprinted from *Cross Currents: The Journal of the Association for Religious and Intellectual Life* by permission. For information on subscribing to *Cross Currents*, contact The Editor at The College of New Rochelle, New Rochelle, NY 10805-2339.

James R. Adams, *The Sting of Death: A study course on death and bereavement* (New York: Seabury, 1971). Used by permission of author.

Herbert T. O'Driscoll, "Aging, a Spiritual Journey," in *Affirmative Aging: A Resource for Ministry*, ed. The Episcopal Society for Ministry on Aging (Minneapolis MN: Winston, 1985) Used by permission of The Episcopal Society on Aging.

Henry C. Simmons, "Visions, Darkness, Light," *Aging and the Human Spirit* 2/2 (Fall 1992).

Kathleen Fischer, *Autumn Gospel: Women in the Second Half of Life* (New York: Paulist, 1995).

Paul B. Maves, "The Church in Community Planning for the Aged," *Pastoral Psychology* 5/46 (September 1954).

chapter 3

THE NEW ME

~❧~

Witness: A Pathway for Spiritual Growth

READING

One of the eminent cultural historians of our time and a self-described eco-theologian, Thomas Berry has written and lectured extensively on the need for humans to move from being a disrupting force in the earth community to being a benign presence. In this selection he explores the role of those who have lived through and shaped the 20th century. Positively or negatively, the elderly are absolutely involved in the total human and the total earth process. These people could have done differently, and our world would have turned out differently.

By its own inner processes, the organic nature of reality is asserting itself in a spontaneous identification of the new roles that individuals and groups are called upon to fulfill at this time. An inner dynamism in the reality of things is asserting itself. (5)

So too with the elderly, it is a question of the elderly themselves being sensitized to their own new situation and to their own role in creating the new order of earthly existence. The elderly alone can create their new roles, even though the assistance of the total society is needed. The elderly are natural leaders of the communities of which they are members. The elderly in the professions have wide control over the professions. The elderly in commerce have extensive control over commerce. So in education, in energy systems, in the arts, and in entertainment, the elderly have widespread influence and extensive control whether in Africa or Asia, Europe or the Americas. Especially in religious and moral affairs, the judgment and influence of the elderly is of supreme importance. Because they have significant influence, they have corresponding responsibilities. The elderly can ruin their own cause. (5)

The image of the elderly as inactive, as nonparticipating observers of the world scene, or as having attained an age simply of enjoyment of life, of detachment from the turmoil of human affairs, is an image that is both illusory and damaging to the elderly. It is illusory because the elderly are absolutely involved in the total human and the total earth process. Elderly participation is not a matter of choice. They participate either as positive contributors or as negative burdens to the community and to the earth. While their mode of participation may be changed, their presence and their insight, their energy, their influence are demanded. For the elderly to remove themselves or to be removed from the earth-human process, is as unacceptable as is the removal of a functional organ from the human body, retiring it before the cessation of bodily life takes place. (5-6)

Any effort of the elderly to escape their proper functioning, or any effort to isolate the active elderly, is destructive in a very direct way to the elderly themselves. They become victimized by the consumer economy. Withdrawal is an indication of the dying down of the will to live on the part of the individual or on the part of the community which finds itself unable to incorporate the elderly into the functional pattern of its life. Above all, the taste for life needs to be sustained on its proper scale and with its proper order of intensity. Generally, efforts at isolation are primarily due to the mechanistic model of the universe and of the human community. The organic model has a place for functional activities that are of value in themselves and not merely in terms of benefits to a consumer society. (6)

For the elderly of the Western industrial countries to make their full contribution to the future, there is need, first of all, that they reflect on the historical role that they have fulfilled throughout this century. The elderly of the present, whatever the benefits they have derived from the industrial developments of the century or whatever the difficulties they have sustained, are the ones who have carried through the great human vision that survives and makes possible the further adjustments that can lessen the damage and enhance the benefits for future generations. The elderly of this generation have carried out a unique role in earth history. Never again will a generation be assigned the historic task of sustaining the human vision at such a moment of transition; for this 20th-century transition of traditional civilizations through a scientific-technological age to an ecological age will never again take place. It will be extended and developed, but the inauguration period that has taken place in this century will not be repeated. It is an irreversible process. While this has been a most conspicuous event in the larger industrial centers, equally conspicuous events have taken place in other countries where the shock of industrial expansion has been compounded by political and economic colonization. Here the difficulty of sustaining a world of human meaning has had its own special manifestations. As elsewhere the elderly in more pastoral or agrarian societies have sustained this difficult period in their own being even as they have been forced to make urgent decisions on behalf of their people and their traditions. (7)

More than others the elderly should have the capacity to identify the general direction of development. They have lived through the entire arc of changes that have taken place. (7)

In this manner they should be able to fulfill their social role as the "wise old men" and the "wise old women" of the present generation. They will thus fulfill their life obligations to themselves, to the society, to their historical destiny, and to the future. Eventually all four of these identify. (7)

The wisdom of the elderly is carried not fundamentally in moralizations or in any philosophical or even religious principles but in the structure of their own being which finds its finest expression in their life stories. This is why the elderly reminisce so much and in their later years become storytellers of the earlier years of their lives and all the particular experiences through which they have passed. While these experiences are individual, they are also the archetypal experiences that reveal the depths of history of the human community and even of the earth process. They provide the perspective needed, the vital sequence whereby the human heritage has been saved from being overwhelmed by the harshness of this particular century. (8)

Here, then, is one of the unique creative roles for the elderly, a role so identified with their own being and the story of their own lives that it should find spontaneous and delightful fulfillment. While only a few of these life stories will be recorded in writing or find their way into print, there exists throughout the human community verbal traditions, group memories of past events. Only when such memories exist can a reliable sense of direction be identified by a community. (9-10)

The elderly are considered endowed with special wisdom because their many years experience has given them a depth of insight into the structure and meaning of the cultural coding that guides the life of the society. They understand the language and rituals better than the others, they know the stories of the society, they have the depth of insight needed for making the major life decisions for the community, they understand the mysterious functioning of the natural world and how best to survive its destructive influence and how best to cooperate with its beneficent powers. In some parts of Africa, the death of an elderly person is considered like the loss of a library. (10)

This cultural coding is of immense importance, for only through this coding do we know how to feed and clothe and shelter ourselves, how to think and speak and act, how to laugh and weep, how to play and sing and dance, how to communicate with the spirit powers of the universe, how to respond intelligently to the mysterious world in which we live. (10-11)

RETREAT

PARTICIPANTS

at least 9 people who have memories going back into the 1920s

FORMAT

5 sessions of 75 minutes each

OBJECTIVES
- To affirm the life experiences of older adults
- To allow older adults to pass on their life experiences to younger generations in their church families

MATERIALS
- newsprint
- markers
- pens
- copies of Berry's article

PREPARATION
1. Invite people of various generations to attend Session 5.
2. Distribute the Berry article to the participants.
3. Place on tables large sheets of newsprint, markers, and pens.

INSTRUCTIONS
Session 1
1. Explain the concept of "story boarding" in which people will share their wisdom through telling their personal stories. Ask the participants to record on newsprint in words, pictures, and diagrams the important events of their worlds during the 1920s (ex: family events, work, social life, inventions, church, music, fashions, elections, politics). (20 minutes)
2. Ask the participants to record on newsprint the important events of their worlds during the 1930s. (20 minutes)
3. Display the 1920s and 1930s reports at different locations in the room.

Session 2
1. Invite the participants to add to the 1920s and 1930s stories recorded on the newsprint posters. (10 minutes)
2. Ask the participants to record on newsprint the important events of their worlds during the 1940s. (20 minutes)
3. Ask the participants to record on newsprint the important events of their worlds during the 1950s. (20 minutes)
4. Display the 1940s and 1950s reports at different locations in the room.

Session 3

1. Invite the participants to add to the 1940s and 1950s stories recorded on the newsprint posters. (10 minutes)
2. Ask the participants to record on newsprint the important events of their worlds during the 1960s. (20 minutes)
3. Ask the participants to record on newsprint the important events of their worlds during the 1970s. (20 minutes)
4. Display the 1960s and 1970s reports at different locations in the room.

Session 4

1. Invite the participants to add to the 1960s and 1970s stories recorded on the newsprint posters. (10 minutes)
2. Ask the participants to record on newsprint the important events of their worlds during the 1980s. (20 minutes)
3. Ask the participants to record on newsprint the important events of their worlds during the 1990s. (20 minutes)
4. Display the 1980s and 1990s reports at different locations in the room.

Session 5

1. Ask the participants to share what they have learned that they want to pass on. Ask them about tears and cheers, fame and shame, hopes dashed and dreams fulfilled. (20 minutes)
2. Ask the participants to circle on the decades posters those memories/lessons learned that they want to pass on to younger generations in the church. (10 minutes)
3. Ask the invited guests (younger generations) to join the group. Seat them according to the decades they represent. Have some elders explain the "fames and shames" of that decade, working from the story-boards. (30 minutes)
4. Close with an event to celebrate the stories of the older generation that are now the stories of the community. Collect the decades posters. (15 minutes)

FOLLOW-UP

1. Have the decades posters transcribed; send copies to participants, asking them to add new insights during the next few
   months.
2. About 2 or 3 months after the organizational meeting, reassemble the group to reread the Berry article and then to discuss
   what they have learned and what they now think is their most
   precious legacy and most pressing responsibility.
3. About 3 or 4 months after the organizational meeting, reassemble the participants to share their new insights.

Service: A Pathway for Spiritual Growth

READING

*For many years Henry Simmons has explored the role of community in
shaping the meaning of old age, whether positively or negatively (by the
absence of any meaning given to old age by the culture). The conference at
which this paper was given was on "Dignity and Old Age." For this
author, both spirituality and community are keys to the possibility and
probability of true dignity in old age.*

The last years of life cannot be adequately described in meager con-
cepts. It is a time of struggle as human frailty threatens to overcome the
quality of this lived life, to overcome the human spirit. (75-76)

I will describe some conditions under which a community focused
on the concerns of those in the last stage of life will successfully affirm
in substantial and sustaining ways what it is to age with dignity. The
three I propose are (a) embracing a dream, (b) supporting a quest for
meaning, and (c) encouraging a quest for freedom. (84)

Embracing a Dream. I have already given two examples of communities that support aging with dignity. [The two examples given in
the article were a Jewish nursing home and the Live Oak Regenerative
Community.] In each case, but in varying degrees, there was a sense
that something was rejected and something was chosen. In the first
case, it was a rejection of institutional time *chronos,* time by the
clock—that leaves institutionalized elders in a chronic state of

waiting—for a meal, for a bath, to have a bed made, to see a TV show. In place of this was put Jewish time—a rhythm of times and seasons that supports people in joy, in grief, in making sense. In the second example what was rejected was a world described by others as being at the bottom of the pecking order, even in nursing home terms—the world of the most frail, the aphasic, those suffering with dementia. In its place was put a way of being that was regenerative—that assumed the possibility of growth, expansion, and healing of self and others. (84-85)

Both dimensions must be present: a collective rejection of the way one is "named" and a collective embracing of a new order. It is not enough to retreat into what is ultimately a "collective privatism"—a community that finds strength and meaning disengaged from the culture. If men and women live long enough they will, in all likelihood, find they no longer fit the picture of what mainstream society judges to be normatively and authentically human—namely, to be productive, to look young, to be physically well and strong. Unless cultural metaphors of aging are confronted, they may ultimately erode the spirit. (85)

Engaged communities recognize that they stand under the oppression of cultural metaphors and images. This is critical if a group is to move from the experience of the *problems* of aging to a dawning sense of agency for individuals and for the group. Genuine dialogue that does not resist the cliches of the culture is the starting point for a recognition that the culture's judgments on old age are not for the sake of those who are experiencing the last stage of life. It is only in this recognition that the possibility of a social order geared to authentic human need can be seen. It is only in this recognition that prophetic images able to support an adequate spirituality can become rich and profuse. (85)

There is no expectation of a quick or dramatic cultural shift. There is, however, a group fearlessness, toughness, and creativity that takes as a starting-point for its own dialogue a recognition and refusal of the norms of a cultural context. (86)

Supporting a Quest for Meaning. The second characteristic of a community committed to aging with dignity is that it support individual quests for meaning. In many ways this point is connected with the previous one. The difference is the focus in this section on the individual's need to work out his or her sense of truth, of making sense, of answering life's "*Whys*." In the context of a larger narrative about human existence in the last stage of life, individuals create personal meaning in ways that differ widely. (86)

Personal interpretations may be as diverse as seeking meaning in contentment from gratification and from one's achievement; enjoying the pleasure of well-earned rest; searching for peak experiences in religious or humanistic exploration; through employment, philanthropy, creative pursuits, or in a dedication to the welfare of others. This latter is particularly sustaining of spirituality in the last stage of life. (86)

Meaning is a common human quest for a map, known or felt, that guides decisions and action, that gives coherence to life, that weaves past, present and future together in continuity, that shapes patterns of behavior in relation to the common and uncommon challenges of life. To seek for meaning is then to ask in some way what is at stake in my life. It is here that we see the connection of aging, spirituality, and community in the last stage of life. To be in the last stage of life is, by definition, to be near the end of one's life. To the extent that one can deal with the fact that there is little time left, finding a personal rightness about life is an increasingly urgent task. Very personal quests of the human spirit will have a better chance of success in communities of dialogue that sustain the quest in substantial and supportive ways. We may see this with special clarity in its absence. (86-87)

"It is difficult to hold to one's own sense of self, to one's own dignity when all around you there is no affirmation of you. At best there may be a patronizing acknowledgment; at worst, you simply do not exist."

"The oppressed old woman is required to be cheerful. But if you are smiling all the time, you acquiesce to being invisible and docile, participating in your own 'erasure'."

"Erasure" is such a powerful image for the threat of nonmeaning that becomes possible when "there is no affirmation of you." This speaks eloquently of the need for a community that supports and sustains spirituality in the last stage of life. (87)

Encouraging a Quest for Freedom. Issues of freedom are not unique to older adults—generally speaking adults of all ages feel they are thinking and acting freely. But for most the parameters of freedom in the earlier adult years are quite narrow, regardless of whether we look at the personal/familial world, the world of peers, or the wider political world. In the personal/familial world, freedom is constrained by commitments, by personal history, by the dynamics of the unconscious, and by larger economic and social forces. In the world of peers, freedom is constrained by trend and fashion, by the need to please, by the tyranny of paycheck and bills, by circles of friends who expect and reinforce group values. In the wider political world, freedom is constrained by fear and social unrest, by the isolation of far suburbs, by media reinforcement of sound-bite thinking, by political processes that seem to offer few real choices. (88)

Some of these constraints lessen with age. Thus, freedom may be more possible in the later years than in the younger years. This is not to romanticize old age. One can be as constrained, as unreflective, and as unfree at 89 as at 39. No blame is intended. Some of the old who have been given few of life's chances are so caught up in the daily requirements of life that they don't tend to look much further. Others have been so socialized into a certain "voice" that their sense of self is cemented to expectations of propriety and role. (88)

Our argument for the growth of the possibility of freedom in the final stage of life runs like this: to the extent that old age is a *terra incognita*, an uncharted world, a place identified by "mainstream" (i.e. the non-old) society as socially irrelevant and whose inhabitants are dispensable; and to the extent that the events and stages of old age inevitably put one in a kind of marginal existence—to that extent the possibility and challenge of freedom grows in old age. (89)

SERVICE PROJECT

PARTICIPANTS

equal number of adults in The New Me stage of life, and older, frail adults

FORMAT

"Partners for Life" organized by a church, a group of churches, a long-term care facility, or a civic organization

OBJECTIVES

- To affirm that it is possible to age with dignity
- To give a sense of meaning to those in The New Me stage of life and to older, frail adults

PREPARATION

1. Identify both groups of participants.
2. Gather information on those residents of the long-term care facility who will participate. If you are not connected with the facility, enlist someone as a resource/support person (ex: the chaplain and/or a social worker) who can provide this information and also assist later as needed.
3. Ask adults of the "new me" stage to record on paper (1) their personal recreational and former career interests and (2) their ideas for service projects with the older adults (ex: read aloud newspapers, magazines, books; write letters; take your partner out of the long-term care facility for worship, meals, etc.; be a prayer partner or a spiritual friend; be a companion on walks or just sit with a partner).
4. Compile and make copies of the service project ideas.
5. Pair adults in the "new me" stage of life with older, more frail adults.
6. Plan an organizational meeting.

INSTRUCTIONS

1. Conduct an organizational meeting at which time partners become acquainted and volunteers receive copies of the service project ideas and voice their concerns/questions.

2. Based on feedback received from the volunteers' forms and in the organizational meeting, plan opportunities for both one-on-one interaction between the partners and large group activities involving all the partners.
3. Schedule some group activities for all the partners 2 weeks after the organizational meeting.
4. Provide for monthly gatherings of the volunteers to share their experiences, receive feedback, and build a sense of community.

Proclamation: A Pathway for Spiritual Growth

READING

Raymond J. Stovich proposes creative and transforming images to help older adults out of stagnation into growth, healing, and fulfillment. His style blends stories with insights from Jungian psychology and Christian faith. Topics include: in wisdom and in grace, remembering, silence, believing, dancing, loving, on archetypes and stereotypes, lessons learned from aging, and working with images.

In weaving and reweaving the elements of our lives we slowly come to the realization that this world is not entirely our "home." The more we come to value the people and things of this life, the more we also see that they are channels for some more profound reality. Thus all of life is a symbol, drawing us forward, out of ourselves, out of ego-centered worlds. The more we appreciate and value this world, the more we realize that it is also a guidepost and inspiration for our souls on their journey to Home. (97-98)

We have learned from the lives of countless seniors that if a person is true to him or her self, something will happen to crack open that personal belief in the importance of the physical, material world. Frequently this comes as a gradual suspicion that there is something "more." Occasionally it comes in the shock of an illness or a sudden vision or paranormal experience. Once it comes, and if we take it seriously, this "opening" will teach us that all of reality is primarily symbolic, that each experience and object will lead us further and further into the Unknown. Soon we will realize that our ideas are indeed our own constructs. They are necessary for our growth and development at certain stages, but they also can keep us from seeing things as they really are. We also learn that "I" am not at all identical to "Ego," that "I" am a symbol for some Mystery. As we pursue life and our world as primarily symbolic, we are led deeper and deeper into direct contact with Reality until these symbols, no longer necessary, fade away and we are "face to face" with whatever Is. Indeed it may be more accurate to say that we are led to the realization that "I" and "Ultimate Reality" no longer exist, but there is only "Is."(100)

The universe is a cosmic dance. For centuries mystics have held this view, and non-mystics have dismissed it as mere poetry. Now non-Newtonian physics is shaking up even the most hard-nosed skeptic. But, really, one does not need to take classes in the history of religion or in particle physics to understand this reality. One simply needs to look at life reflectively, to see its patterns develop, shift, and reconfigure. Exploring moments from the lives of the elderly has amply illustrated that a touch of humor and some clear-eyed honesty is all that's needed to begin the Dance. There seem to be two themes unifying these diverse lessons learned from working with the elderly and reflecting upon that work and their lives. First of all, human life is situated in a "place in-between." We are not simply physical beings, tied to mother earth and the matter from which we are made. On the other hand we are not pure spirit, free to roam about at will through time and space. We are both physical and immaterial, simultaneously living in both realms, or more accurately living in a place in-between both realms. (102)

The second theme has to do with one of the unique ways in which our in-between nature manifests itself to us, namely, that the human life is also the symbolic life. As previously indicated, it is important to distinguish a symbol from a sign. A sign has one clear "meaning" which it represents. A traffic sign indicates the activity of stopping, or going, etc. A symbol, on the other hand, does not simply convey information. A symbol is an image which also conveys the living reality of what it symbolizes. A wedding ring is not simply a sign of a marriage. After 20 years of shared life, that ring recreates those moments, of joy, frustration, elation, love, etc. (103)

Working with the elderly also suggests a few reflections about lifestyle. The lessons learned in this work suggest that in order to live a happy and fully alive life, the symbolic life of an "in-between being," we must integrate the following points into our daily lives. (103)

First of all, we need to live as much as possible in the present moment. This sounds simple, but in fact is rather difficult to do. Much of nonsleeping time is spent in the past or the future. Reminiscence differs from daydreaming about the past. Daydreaming is mostly an unconscious activity. Reminiscence brings a reflective awareness of the past, building a sense of interiority, of soul, by using our memories as symbols. Daydreaming about the future, as opposed to consciously planning or fantasizing, usually does little more than reinforce our own neediness. One of the effects of living in the present is to build an openness which will be a source of joy and ecstacy as well as a source of sorrow and pain, for it will expose us to the multiple dimensions of life as it is lived around us and on this planet. As we become moved by our own sufferings and the sufferings and struggles of others, our openness can become a powerful and never depleting source of compassion. (103)

If we are to live the symbolic life, we must learn to live a life of interiority. Unlike signs which usually shout their messages, symbolic images are normally shy and reserved beings. Their power is not in a message but in their operations upon one's inner life. In order to allow these images to accomplish their tasks, we need to stop our frenetic pace. We need leisure and times of silence, times of introversion, of directing our attention inward. Unfortunately this attitude is diametrically opposed to the frenetic, extroverted lifestyle of the modern world, a world in which everything is, or will be, knowable and doable. Yet symbols quietly cry out of the mysteries of life and the Mystery behind or beyond them. To fulfill our humanity, we must take time and heed their cry. (104)

Finally, we must learn to live with paradox. The simplest way of stating this is to say that nothing is ever what it seems to be. For instance, something I do to make myself feel good actually exacerbates my deepest wounds. A seemingly heartless act becomes a great moment of compassion. The reality of human life, that strange mixture of spirits and matter, is that, at each and every moment, many realities are occurring simultaneously. Understanding this requires a certain flexibility of mind, again a trait opposed to the trends of our current culture. Today we want hard facts, a byproduct of our materialistic society, and the machines we use to process facts can deal with only "yes or no" statements. And as life becomes faster and faster, and more complicated and ambiguous, we look for a simple way out. And yet the glorious truth of human nature is that we are multidimensioned, symbolic beings. Life is a mystery in that life *isn't* what it usually appears to be. At the very heart of its being is a pulsing and dynamic Mystery. (104)

SERMON

TOPIC
"Steadfast love surrounds those who trust in the Lord."

SCRIPTURE
Psalm 32

FOCUS
When we acknowledge and confess the "sin" of being old, God's love becomes a place of deliverance and a source of happiness.

FUNCTION
To reassure elders of God's love so that they can live fully.

THEME
In contemporary culture it is a "sin" to be old. Even the old feel lessened by the adding of years. When the old "confess" this sin and accept God's everpresent love for them as they are, they will find in God a place of deliverance. There, in the presence of God, they can become open and compassionate. Without abandoning their creative roles in shaping the present, they can live a life of interiority in the presence of God. They can live with the conviction that at the heart of everyday ordinariness is a pulsing and

dynamic mystery. As a way of moving to this mystery, they can learn to live in the present moment, without daydreaming about the past or future, but with a reflective awareness of the past and an openness to the future.

Teaching: A Pathway for Spiritual Growth

READING

Eugene C. Bianchi sees aging as a human phenomenon and spiritual challenge rather than as a series of unfortunate ills and inevitable losses. His unique contribution is the way he encourages us to see death as a life-affirming challenge.

To be truthful from the start, we should admit that there is no fully adequate way to prepare for one's own death. (150)

Admittedly, there is a certain fear, perhaps even terror, involved in allowing intimations of our own death into our minds and hearts. (156)

At the heart of the development of one's own spirituality through reflection on one's finitude is a deeper experience of faith. Faith is frequently misunderstood as a collection of beliefs connected with certain moral practices and rituals. Yet faith must be distinguished from these religious manifestations. Faith is an attitude and act of profound trust in the face of death with its ultimate threat of annihilating all meaning. Faith is an action of releasing the walled-off self into communion with a benevolent and sustaining Reality that pervades a death-oriented cosmos. In its depths, it is a kind of letting-go that only that person can perform who understands from his or her own life the final transitoriness of all things. (159)

Finally, such faith keeps us from falling into the paralysis and disintegration that afflict many who are not able to cope with the indications of their own aging and death. A kind of psychological death occurs when an individual tries to deny the signs of finitude in neurotic modes of withdrawal from life or of heedless plunging into youthful activities. Such a person is clinging fearfully to life as a possession to be defended against death, rather than as a gift to be shared to the end. Faith gives one the courage to break through those temptations and infuse life with hope and meaning in ever-richer ways as death approaches. (160)

Meditation on personal death can also become an occasion for deepening our friendships and intimacies. When we become conscious of unhealthy defenses against death, in faith we can release some of our fearfulness. As we do this, our attitude toward family and friends can change; we can permit more of our true selves, with our illusions and vulnerabilities, to appear. (164)

In the process of enriching our friendships as we encounter our own finitude, there is a paradoxical joining of pain and joyfulness. It is painful to become more accepting of our weaknesses, hostilities, and self-deceptions; yet, when we have been educated in the school of death, we can also regard more lightly matters that we might otherwise take too seriously. (164)

Refined in the crucible of their own sufferings and sacrifices, elders are gradually purified of egotism but develop fuller self-esteem. Their trials teach them greater truthfulness that lessens self-deception and makes them wise guides for others. They seem able to infuse their lives with quality time, even when the quantity of sand is smaller in the top of the hourglass. Instead of the inflexibility sometimes associated with the old, these elders go through a self reidentification process. This means fulfilling some of the needs and desires that went unrealized in earlier years. To summarize these gracious developments in such older people, we can say that in the very face of death they experience a greater freedom from the fear of death. (165-66)

Though we are certain that we will die, the actual event will always remain something of a surprise. This is an important note to keep before us as we address proximate preparation for death. (168)

As our fear of the dying process diminishes, we become sources of security and even hope for the dying. Helping others to die with dignity and hope can be enhanced by a spirit of faith. (174)

Reflection on death, especially on one's own death, in long-term or in proximate scenarios, can enrich the aging process. Contemplation of personal death can spur one on to make the most of the present, whatever one's age. Such contemplation is not an exercise in morbidity for those who have started to work through the transitional crises of midlife. My death, while always fear-inspiring in some ways, can also be seen as part of the natural cycle of all living creatures. Christians can learn a corrective lesson from naturalists on this point. (175)

A comprehensive view of death for persons of faith places it within the natural, God-established order of the universe. Acceptance of this mode of coming to be and of passing on becomes an act of fidelity to God's providence. Such reflection helps us develop a mystic sense of belonging to a greater whole, of being part of a trustworthy purpose in the world as we make our particular contribution to what English philosopher Alfred North Whitehead called the "creative advance." (176)

It may seem strange to speak of death as a final celebration of life. Yet that is precisely the paradox of faith. Perhaps the greatest grace we will ever experience is that of celebrating what has been and what is, as we draw near to our death. This is a special gracing for which our whole life can be a preparation. To celebrate is to rejoice for having experienced life with its pains and joys, to be glad that we have helped our survivors to preserve and nourish the beautiful, fragile gift of life into yet another season. (178)

GROUP DISCUSSION

TOPIC
   "Called to Live and Next to Die"

PARTICIPANTS
   people who recognize that, generationally, they are the next to die

FORMAT
   60-90 minutes

OBJECTIVES
   • To name the experience of realizing that one is now "the elder"
   • To name the event in which one realized that he or she is "next in line" to die (i.e., no one stands between you and death)
   • To reflect on one's own death, naming the fears and the faith

- To commit to a "death-recognizing faith" that enables us to deepen friendships and commitments

MATERIALS
- newsprint
- markers
- copies of Bianchi's article

PREPARATION

Distribute the Bianchi article to participants.

INSTRUCTIONS
1. Ask the participants to share an experience in which they recognized their new status as "the elder" (ex: being placed at the head of the table; being addressed in a certain way; being left out of certain decision-making processes). Ask them to discuss their feelings and insights. (20-25 minutes)
2. Ask the participants to name an event or occasion in which dawned the realization or implications of being "next in line." Ask them to discuss their feelings and insights. (10-15 minutes)
3. Ask the participants to name fears about death that might be common for those who know that death is likely to come next to someone in their generation. Record these on newsprint. (10-15 minutes)
4. Ask the participants to name personally what keeps them accepting of the inevitability of death. Match these with the fears of death they listed earlier. (20-25 minutes)
5. Close with a ritual of dedication to life-enhancing relationships and commitments. See suggestions below: (5-10 minutes)

- Invite the participants to sit in a circle, with a lighted candle in their midst. Distribute copies of the 3 phrases they will say later and explain their use. Open with a few moments of silence and then a prayer.
- Each participant, in turn, says, "With faith in God's mercy (or kindness, or compassion, or . . .), I take my place as an elder in my family and in the community."

- Each participant, in turn, says, "I recognize I will die someday, although I do not know the day nor the hour. Now, in life, I dedicate myself to deepen my relationships and commitments."
- Observe 2 or 3 minutes of silence, giving the participants time to absorb the importance of the moment.
- Close with a prayer, a blessing, a passing of the peace, and a dismissal.

Prayer: A Pathway for Spiritual Growth

READING

Susan Coupland addresses the special concern of parishioners who seek to begin or to renew their lives of prayer later in life. She makes suggestions on helpful reading and taking private retreats, offers examples of appropriate short prayers, and gives advice on ways to cope with the physical limitations of aging when they arise along the spiritual journey.

I felt that the all-important thing was to learn to pray, both in church with the new family and also at home in my own way. But we have to accept that learning to pray in later life is a different thing from learning early in life. I have the impression that Christians who have enjoyed long years of church membership learn the lessons of prayer in a gradual, natural way, almost imperceptibly integrating a lifetime of experiences into their prayers. But after we retire, time is short in which to learn the greatest thing in life—to search for God and to try to know him and to love him. Many great saints who have given up a whole lifetime to prayer, have said that even after 50 years they were still beginners in prayer. But that need not deter us, even though we are well on into our 70s or 80s. The parable of the late-comers to the vineyard (Matt 20:1-16) is a plain answer to any we may raise. (11)

God most certainly wants us in his vineyard, but I am sure it is important not to overstrain by trying to make up for lost time. Learning to pray and to love God is not something we can hurry; we must be prepared to be patient and to make haste slowly. Nor must we be discouraged by the saintly certainty of many books about prayer, often

written by people in religious communities who have given much
time to prayer. We must go to God in the way he points out for us as
very ordinary people. Though we may have neglected him and disappointed him in the past, be very sure that he will not disappoint us
now if we really trust him. (11)

Most of us, after we are about 75, experience increasing loneliness.
Friends die; others become housebound or find traveling difficult.
People find us less interesting, and so friends come to see us less frequently. This makes life less interesting and exciting. There may be a
deeper loneliness that we find difficult to communicate. We know
that very soon we shall have no part in this world, and so it becomes
very precious. How can we bear to leave the ever changing beauty of
the landscape from the kitchen window, that lovely willow tree
through which the sunlight falls like drops of golden rain, the garden
we have created over the years with love and care, the sitting room on
which we have implanted our personality and the little gifts all round
the room, each representing a friendship. Will there be someone to
help us when the time comes, or shall we have to make the journey
quite alone? If we still have our marriage partner, the unspoken question is often there—which of us will go first? (30-31)

We can talk freely to God about these fears and depressions. We
should try to listen to his loving reassurance as we find it perhaps in
Psalms 46 or 23, in the first few verses of St John's Gospel, chapter 14,
or in the wonderful end of the 8th chapter of the Epistle to the
Romans. (31)

It sometimes happens that before long we know that we have a
friend in the room, someone standing very close to us. We can talk to
him. We can break down and cry in his arms. We can share a joke with
him. We can say anything we like, and we can lean on his strength
when all our own is ebbed away. Even if not a single word is framed,
we can hold out our hands to him in love and know that we are praying. In old age we must accept that often we shall have strength for no
more than that, and it is all he wants. (32)

At first our prayer concentrates on ourselves. It has to be that way
because we have a relationship to establish. But if we continue to let

the relationship grow, we shall naturally and without any difficulty begin to pray for those we love. Then we shall find out that this is not enough, and we shall start to pray for those we find it hard to forgive. The next step will be to realize that there are some who find it diffi-cult to forgive us. It will all happen naturally and step by step, if we open ourselves to God's Holy Spirit. All the time there are new com-panions in our journey of prayer even though we may not meet them in the flesh. (32)

Elderly people tend to live much more in the past than they for-merly did and usually to dwell on happy memories and to talk about them a great deal. Reminiscing may or may not be a bad habit of old people, but it is a fairly inevitable development. Many of us find that our memory of what happened a week ago can be poor, but memories of a quarter or half a century ago can be very vivid indeed. For the elderly who, in old age, accept a definite commitment to become a disciple of our Lord, the past can become a problem, even though there may be thousands of happy memories and a lifetime of fruitful and selfless activity. The latecomer into the church is not always wel-come, and will probably feel that he has failed our Lord during the best years of his life. (58)

Both for the new disciple and for the long-term Christian, a good, honest look at the past can do no harm. I have met one very good teacher of prayer who suggested dividing up one's life into 7-year peri-ods, consciously recollecting the special blessings of each period and then giving thanks for them. For some this may not be easy, for life is a whole, a flowing stream, sometimes meandering peacefully and hap-pily, sometimes disturbed by eddies and unexpected currents. A neat design of life does not fit the experience of many people and in that case it may be better to go back to the simple words of the first chap-ter—"Just as I am." It will help us to recollect that God must have been accepting us, just as we are and forgiving us all through the years when we did not know him. (59)

Nevertheless, the fact of past sin and guilt may distress us. Yet an obsessive sense of guilt is wrong; it is stultifying and a denial of God's omnipotence and love. We have to look honestly at past sin and to love ourselves in spite of it. It is a weakness to concentrate too long on introspective self-examination. We can't forget the past; nor does God. But we can accept it and ask his forgiveness and so strengthen our relationship with him and our love for him. If God forgives us, as he always does when a sinner is penitent, then we, too, must do his will and forgive ourselves. If we have suffered unduly at the hands of others or through harsh circumstances, we must also forgive what these things have done to us. Then we can reach forward to the new growth that lies ahead of us. (59)

In physical weakness it is sometimes possible to concentrate pleasure on one simple thing and, perhaps, to fall into restful sleep while doing so. It is another form of thankfulness and one to which, in old age, we might train ourselves. It is useless, when ill, to try to make prayers which put a strain on strength. Far better to give thanks for one small blessing and to make an offering of love through it. (66-67)

SERMON

TOPIC
"God's Work of Art"

SCRIPTURE
Ephesians 2:4-10, read with the Coupland article in mind

FOCUS
Because God is rich in mercy and loves us so much, we can recognize and celebrate that the elders among us are God's work of art.

FUNCTION
To celebrate the mercy and love of God in the lives of the elders among us, recognizing them as God's work of art.

THEME
Today we recognize the members of this congregation who are old. We affirm that they have value because of God's enduring love for them. To us they may be simply living in a time of lowered expectations and decline. But the Scriptures remind us that they

are God's work of art. God is not finished with them yet. They are still called to do the things God created them to do. They have in God a new future, not just a long past. They are witnesses to the immense resources of God's grace and kindness. Our recognition of our elders today is not for what they did in the past, but for who they are in Christ today.

RITUAL

In the week before the service, invite each of the elders who will be recognized to write on paper a phrase or verse from the Bible that sustains and uplifts them. Incorporate these verses into an artistic typeset or handwritten offering; make copies for everyone in the congregation. At the time of recognition, call each elder by name. Tell the congregation that the elders have a gift to give them. Have two people read the verses slowly, alternating readers. Say a blessing over this cooperative "work of art" and distribute copies throughout the congregation.

Community: A Pathway for Spiritual Growth

READING

Jane Thibault is convinced that "the development of an intense, mutual, love relationship with God is the primary spiritual task of later life" (19). Her book is written for the spiritually discontent older adult and deals with the inner work the author considers to be the spiritual life task of the mature adult. The style of the book is at once conversational and informed.

God is calling you, an old person, out of your grave. You are well prepared for your own, personal resurrection because in addition to the gift of God's presence, you and your peers alone have been given radical freedom. The *radical freedom of age*. You are what the scientists call a critical mass, a group of people who exist in large enough numbers to make a difference in the world because more than the energy of one person is needed for this work. (23)

Your Father has called you into being to experience, to share an incredible, perpetually expanding abundance of life—God's own life lived in loving unity with the Son and the Spirit. This abundance of life is not given as our society gives—just to children and young adults. God's abundance is for all ages, for all stages of the life span. God wants to gift you, to energize you, with this abundance. God wants to pour into you each second of each day of your life gifts that will ravish you, that will sweep you off your feet, that will envelop you with love and joy and peace. God's great anguish comes from your barriers, your inability or refusal to become aware that these gifts exist for you. They are there for you: there for the asking and for the receiving. (38)

Once we become aware of and acknowledge the gift-nature of our lives we will begin to turn radically toward God with increasingly open hearts, minds, and hands. Trusting in the benevolence of God's love, perhaps for the first time, we will tentatively start to allow ourselves to be loved. A childlike openness to God and all the gifts God desires to give us and to others through us will become our new life stance. (62)

What are we supposed to do with an invitation like this—an invitation to experience God's presence, to live the family life of the Trinity? How do we prepare ourselves to respond to such an incredible gift? (73)

Here are some formal steps we can take to facilitate our response. We are first invited to become *aware* of the reality of the presence of God within us. Do we really believe (but not necessarily feel or experience) the teachings of scripture—that the kingdom of God, that God's self, is within us, that the Father as creativity, the Son as love, and the Spirit as the energy that marries them and then infuses love and creativity into the world dwell in us and that we are part of that life? If we can say even a hesitant yes to this question, even if all we can manage is the desire to believe, we are preparing ourselves to receive this gift. (74)

Our next task is to accept the second part of the gift: we must *acknowledge* the fact that the awareness and experience of this presence is available to us if we desire it strongly enough. We must also be willing to share it with others, for we must be willing to become present to others, just as God is to us. (74)

Next we must *ask* for this gift with great singleness of desire combined with hope, belief, and trust that it will be given because God wants to give knowledge and experience of this love to us. (74)

Once we receive this gift (and it will be given, but in God's own time and dependent on our preparedness), we must accept it with an attitude of appreciation, gratefulness, and inner poverty. We must know that we have not earned this gift, nor can we give it to ourselves. Because it is pure gift, it flows from the generosity of the love of God for us. (74)

Next, we must nurture this ever-deepening, ever-expanding, love relationship with the Father, Son, and Spirit within our hearts and in the hearts of our neighbors, for this love is given not just to us alone; it is meant always to flow through us and outward toward the world. (74)

Finally, we must keep in mind that at some point we may be asked to let go, to relinquish our awareness and enjoyment of this relationship. Because the joys of this relationship can be so intense, especially for people who are gifted with a more emotional personality type, there can arise the temptation to love the fact of being in relationship more than concentrating purely and totally on the One whom we love. When we enjoy the relationship more than the Loved One, we are really focusing selfishly on ourselves and our feeling state. Believe it or not, we can even become greedy for the experience of relationship with God! The old masters call this spiritual gluttony. (74)

They say that when you say yes, when you open yourself to Loving Presence—the presence of God, yourself, and other people—with your whole heart and mind and soul and body, you will fall in Love. In love with Love. Because Love lives in you and embraces you and has been pouring love unceasingly into your entire being from the moment of your conception. And while you were being knitted in your mother's womb. And on the day of your birth. And at the moment of your first awareness of your own self. (82)

If you say yes to this invitation to love in whatever ways Love manifests Love's Self to you, you will enter into an affair of the soul which will continue all the days of your life. It will awaken you and enliven you to the loving presence of God and all of God's creation. You will join with others throughout the ages on a journey both inward and outward, to the still point of the turning world as T. S. Eliot puts it, the place of unity where all things, all persons, all meanings converge and rest in contemplative appreciation and enjoyment of each other. Because God's Self is manifested so uniquely in every person, this journey will be different for each human being, yet it has a direction that is common to most people who respond to the love of God for them. (84)

Eventually, at some point that can never be predicted or planned, you will find yourself called into the deep and vast solitude of your own soul where God will speak to your heart. There God will gently tell you how you need to grow, what you need to do (or not do), how you need to be, how you can respond in order to prepare yourself to deepen your awareness of love and to receive even more love. God's voice will be understood by you in whatever way you learn best— through people, events, reading, places, inner promptings, intuitions, feelings. What God communicates to you always calls you to expand, to go beyond both the comfortable and the painful limits you have set for yourself. God is now inviting you to become more of who you really are. (85)

GROUP ENCOUNTER

PARTICIPANTS
   older adults in the "new me" stage of life

FORMAT
   4 sessions, 60 minutes each

OBJECTIVES
   • To walk "new me" older adults through Thibault's steps as described in her article
   • To introduce participants to different ways of praying

- To lead participants to experience a sense of community with one another that is potentially unlike another community in which they have been a member

MATERIALS
- Bible
- copies of Thibault's article

PREPARATION
Distribute copies of the Thibault article to the participants.

INSTRUCTIONS
Week 1
1. To increase awareness of the reality of the presence of God, lead the participants in a *lectio divina* exercise using John 15:1-5. Have the participants find a comfortable sitting position, keeping their feet flat on the floor, and then to breathe in and out 2-3 deep cleansing breaths. Read the Scripture passage slowly. Read it again after a brief pause. (10 minutes)
2. Allow the participants to commune in silence with the Scripture passage. (20 minutes)
3. Invite the participants to share voluntarily and in confidence their experiences of silent meditation. (30-35 minutes)
4. Ask participants to enter into *lectio divina* with any Scripture reading during the next week and to record their experiences in a journal for possible sharing in the next session. (5 minutes)
Week 2
1. Invite participants to share the prayer experiences they had in the intervening week, emphasizing that they should not compare their experience with that of others. Invite them to look at the myriad of ways God can be present in people's lives. If there are some members who experienced God's absence, lead into a discussion about how God can be present when seemingly absent. (50 minutes)

2. Ask participants to pray for God's presence during the next week, perhaps in unexpected ways, and to record their experiences in a journal for possible sharing in the next session. Suggest resources on different types of prayer. (10 minutes)

Week 3

1. Invite participants to share the prayer experiences they had in the intervening week, emphasizing that they should not compare their experience with that of others. Perhaps some will become receptive to other ways of acknowledging God's presence through the sharing. (45 minutes)

2. Ask participants to consider prayerfully and to accept God's presence in their lives as it is made manifest to them during the next week, even if it feels like absence. If some are unable to do this, lead into a discussion of presence and absence. Suggest resources on different types of prayer. Encourage journaling for possible sharing in the next session. (15 minutes)

Week 4

1. Invite participants to share the prayer experiences they had in the intervening week, emphasizing that they should not compare their experience with that of others. (30 minutes)

2. Have the participants discuss ways that their relationship with God can continue to grow with a sense of inner poverty. If they need prompting, you might suggest continuing contemplative prayer. There are also different ways that the nurturing can happen through the outward expression of the gift of God's presence. Emphasize that the outward expression comes from the new or heightened sense of community that each participant has with God. If there is interest, invite the group to a sharing session in 3-4 months. (30 minutes)

Source Notes

Thomas Berry, "Preface," in *Aging: Spiritual Perspectives,* ed. Francis V. Tiso (Lake Worth FL: Sunday Publications, 1982). Used by permission of the book's editor.

Henry C. Simmons, "Spirituality and Community in the Last Stage of Life," in *Dignity and Old Age,* ed. Robert Disch, Rose Dobrof, and Harry R. Moody (New York: Haworth Press, Inc., 1988) 73-91.

S. Healey, "Growing to Be an Old Woman: Aging and Agism," *in Worlds of Difference: Inequality in the Aging Experience,* ed. E. P. Stoller and R. C. Gibson (Thousand Oaks CA: Pine Forge Press, 1994) 83.

Raymond J. Stovich, *In Wisdom and Grace* (Kansas City MO: Sheed and Ward, 1988). Reprinted with permission of *The National Catholic Reporter Publishing Company.*

Eugene C. Bianchi, "Death Preparation as Life Enhancement," in *Affirmative Aging: A Resource for Ministry,* ed. The Episcopal Society for Ministry on Aging (Minneapolis MN: Winston, 1985). Used by permission of The Episcopal Society for Ministry on Aging.

Copyright © 1985 by Susan Coupland. All rights reserved. Reprinted from *Beginning to Pray in Old Age,* published by Cowley Publications, 28 Temple Place, Boston, MA 02111. (1-800-225-1534)

A Deepening Love Affair. Copyright © 1993 by Jane Marie Thibault. Used by permission of Upper Room Books.

chapter 4

LIKE IT OR NOT

~~~❧❧~~~

Service: A Pathway to Spiritual Growth

READING

The purpose of the Friends Club, as described by Molly Tully and Joan Turner, is to provide an intimate and caring therapeutic environment for socially isolated men in the early and middle stages of Alzheimer's Disease. Unique in that it is a men's club instead of a day-care program, Friends Club has served more than 300 men in the greater Washington community since its founding in 1990. The concept of this club is relatively simple to implement and can be replicated in other contexts.

Purpose. The purpose of Friends Club is to provide an intimate and caring therapeutic environment for socially isolated men in the early and middle stages of Alzheimer's Disease—an option for men who do not choose to attend a traditional adult day-care program or as a supplement to such attendance. Friends Club is a place where men can enjoy the company of their peers in a relaxed, nonjudgmental setting, thus reinforcing their self-esteem and providing a respite for their caregivers. (Foreword)

The unique feature of Friends Club is that it is a *bona fide* men's club, not a day-care program. Membership is made up of approximately 15 retired men, 9 of whom have Alzheimer's Disease, 6 of whom [the volunteers] do not. (1)

The concept of a social club for men with Alzheimer's Disease was formed during a lunch shared by two wives who had become acquainted through a support group sponsored by the Alzheimer's Association of Greater Washington. Both were concerned about the social isolation, lack of activity, and wounded egos of their husbands as they struggled in their own ways to accept and cope with the reality of increasing cognitive impairment and the abrupt end of their highly successful professional lives. These wives also shared the need for regular respite from their caregiver roles. Both had investigated various adult day-care programs and concluded that none was appropriate for their husbands, who were desperately clinging to their professional identities and searching for meaningful ways to relate to society. Both men were in a state of denial that anything was wrong, and they did not want to be considered impaired. A traditional adult day-care program simply was not an option at this time. What then would be appropriate? The idea of forming a social club for men with Alzheimer's seemed a natural outgrowth from the sharing of these two concerned wives. (2)

Premises. The subsequent development of the Friends Club has been described as "instinct driven." Guidance from Alzheimer's professionals and adult day-care managers has been and continues to be critical to the ongoing success of the program. The original concept, however, was created from the following convictions:

- that men particularly enjoy the company of other men, but that as the disease gradually diminishes their capabilities Alzheimer's men generally withdraw from former associates and become depressed and socially isolated
- that men with Alzheimer's Disease still retain for the most part their physical coordination and aesthetic and emotional senses, and it is possible to plan activities which engage these yet do not rely on cognitive functioning, thus ensuring a successful experience
- that membership which includes unimpaired retired male volunteers as well as Alzheimer's men lends authenticity to the men's club idea

- that a men's club format automatically dictates appropriate activities
- that to minimize confusion and maximize a sense of belonging, club attendance should be limited to a maximum of 10 or 12 people on any one day
- that it is possible to tailor an activity program around the individual strengths, losses and personal interests of a small group of men with Alzheimer's (2)

Participants. The first challenge, of course, was to persuade these socially insecure men [the 4 Alzheimer's participants who comprised the charter membership of Friends Club] to join the club! To introduce the men to each other, a dinner party was held in the home of one of the couples. [. . .] This very successful evening served as a useful reference when a letter of invitation to join the club was received shortly thereafter. No pressure was exerted, only a gentle suggestion that they might find some enjoyment in getting together. (4-5)

Recruiting Volunteers. Originally it was thought that the volunteers would rotate so they would not feel compelled to come every week. A survey was circulated asking which Fridays they preferred. It was found that almost all wanted to come every week unless something unforeseen kept them away. Quoting from one volunteer, "After coming a few times to the Friends Club I found a real sociability and solidarity building with the others in the group. Coming to the club has become a pleasure." (5)

Volunteer training is an important element in any program dealing with dementia. The volunteers have preferred "on-the-job" training under the direction of the professional program director, supplemented by reading materials provided for them in the club library. (6)

Activities. What kinds of activities do men enjoy doing together? "Club men" report that they most enjoy the opportunity for informal conversation and regular socializing with their peers. In our effort to pattern the Friends Club after a "typical men's club," we settled on an early format of spending the first part of the morning in relaxed conversation. Once the group is seated, the director usually steers the conversation to a topic of interest, whether it is World War II, old-fashioned cars, telephones, movie stars, baseball, or "this day in history." Occasionally word games or crossword puzzles (on a poster) are attempted to stimulate thinking processes. Trivia games are popular. There are tables set up for dominos or checkers for any who want to play (always with a volunteer), and videos and slides of members' trips are sometimes shown. Field trips to nearby places of interest are scheduled at least once a month. Every month or so, the children from the pre-primary school next door come over for a program of intergenerational activity: making candy apples at Halloween, exchanging valentines, hunting Easter eggs, making Christmas tree decorations, or just singing familiar songs together. The men appear to enjoy the spontaneous and nonjudgmental presence of the 4-5 year olds, and vice versa! Arts for the Aging, a nonprofit group which provides artists, dancers, sculptors, mimes, etc., has been used on several occasions, some more successfully than others. Lunch, of course, is the highlight of the day, a time to enjoy the food prepared by the volunteers and members themselves, and a time to exchange informal chit-chat until the wives arrive to pick them up. (7)

Community Service. A familiar and painful complaint from victims of Alzheimer's Disease—perhaps especially men—is that they are unable to find "meaningful work" to fill their time. One of the most successful activities at Friend's Club has been the community service project which happens each week. Martha's Table, a soup kitchen and day-care program for children, is the beneficiary of 100 cheese sandwiches prepared and delivered each week by Friends Club. Sandwich making is a communal assembly line activity shared by everyone. Tasks are divided and carefully assigned so that every member experiences success and pleasure at being able to "do his job." One of the field trips the men took was to see and tour Martha's Table when delivering their sandwiches so that they had the satisfaction of seeing that they are indeed engaged in meaningful volunteer work. Through this experience of giving to the less fortunate, the participants' own sense of self-worth is enhanced. (8)

SERVICE PROJECT

PARTICIPANTS

15 people minimum

FORMAT

2 sessions of 60 minutes each; 1 session of 60-90 minutes, spanning 3 weeks

OBJECTIVES

Week 1
- To demonstrate a clear understanding of the Tully/Turner article
- To initiate a process for assessing needs and strengths
- To match needs with the strengths of those who wish to serve

Week 2
- To arrive at a consensus on needs
- To begin a process of identifying strengths

Week 3
- To initiate project implementation at whatever level of commitment the group has expressed or to debrief the process and bring it to closure if the individuals in the group have not indicated a willingness to commit to a project

MATERIALS
- newsprint
- markers
- copies of Tully's/Turner's article

PREPARATION

Week 1
1. Distribute the Tully/Turner article to the participants.
2. Place newsprint and markers on each table.

Week 2
Place newsprint and markers on each table.

Week 3
Place newsprint and markers on each table.

INSTRUCTIONS

Week 1

1. Form groups of 4-5. Have each group discuss the Tully/Turner article and on newsprint to identify the problem, initial insight, and steps taken to realize the project. (20-25 minutes)

2. Reassemble the large group. Ask each small group to report its findings. Engage in general discussion. (10-15 minutes)

3. Return to small groups. Have each group recommend steps that the large group could take to identify needs in the congregation or community. (20-25 minutes)

4. Ask each small group to list on newsprint its findings. Lead the group to decide what steps need to be taken and who will be responsible for each step. Set a date for the next meeting. (15 minutes)

Week 2

1. In the large group, hear reports on the needs identified in the previous meeting. Group these needs appropriately, filling in details as needed, and print them on newsprint. Print on newsprint those resources needed to implement a response to each need. (10-15 minutes)

2. Form groups of 4-5. Have each group identify and rank in order from most to least intense the strengths for service of the men's group. Emphasize that this is a brainstorming process and that the group is not yet making any commitment to action. (20-25 minutes)

3. Return to the large group. Ask each small group to report its findings. Come to a consensus and write this on newsprint. (10-15 minutes)

4. Schedule the next meeting. Ask participants to spend at least 2, 30-minute periods during the following week on this activity: (1) Write the need and strength that seem most appropriate for the group to address. (2) Indicate the commitment of time, energy, and talent you would be willing to make. (10 minutes)

<u>Week 3</u>

1. In the large group, record on newsprint the needs and strengths identified as most appropriate for the group to address. If there is a wide range of responses, the group should discuss each opinion thoroughly and try to arrive at either a consensus or rank-ordering. Identify projects that might meet the need, based on the group's strengths. (10-15 minutes)

2. Form groups of 4-5. Identify on newsprint the resources that would be needed to implement each project identified in the large group. (20-25 minutes)

3. Return to the large group. Ask each small group to report its findings. (5-10 minutes)

4. Ask each participant to assess for himself, in the light of what he wrote during the week, a project to which he is willing to commit himself. Examples of commitment might range from "nothing right now," to "seeking other men or groups to participate," to "gathering further information," to "finding if other groups are engaged in similar projects," to "being part of a design team." Ask that these commitments be recorded on newsprint, signed, and given to the leader. (15-20 minutes)

5. During a break, tally the results. (5 minutes)

6. Return to the large group. If there is no consensus about a project the participants are willing to engage in now, debrief the process and disband the group. If there is consensus about a project, set a time for a meeting when implementation will begin. (10-15 minutes)

Proclamation: A Pathway to Spiritual Growth

READING

Kathleen Fischer shows how Christian faith can transform the later years of life. She presents an inclusive definition of spirituality as "the ultimate ground of all our questions, hopes, fears, and loves; our efforts to deal creatively with retirement and to find a purpose for our lives after our family has been raised; our struggles with the loss of a spouse; or the move from a family home of many years; questions of self-worth and fear of reaching out to make new friendships; the discovery of new talents, deeper peace, wider boundaries of love" (9).

We cannot learn to understand aging if we undervalue or over-value its realities, or if we simply try to make it appear as much like midlife or youth as possible. (3)

The fact is that aging is *both* descent and ascent, *both* loss and gain. This is true of growth at every stage of the life cycle: childhood, adolescence, midlife, and old age. Time is both life and death. (4)

Winter reveals those things that summer conceals. We can see farther and with clearer vision. Paths that were clogged with vines or leaves in summer and fall open up, and we can walk in places not possible in other seasons. There is an inner life and awakening: beneath the shell of the bud is sap in gestation, and the colors of spring tinge the nudity of winter. (5)

What are the graces of winter? The word "grace" has many meanings. So, too, the graces of the later years take many forms. We describe beauty of movement as grace. The rhythm of old age may be slower than that of youth, but it can reveal a new kind of beauty, one refined by experience. Graciousness and mercy are other aspects of grace. Old age can be a time of larger love and compassion, of attitudes of good will and thoughtfulness toward others. We call a temporary exemption or reprieve a grace period. Since we all stand under the certain sentence of death, the gift of several additional years of life is such a period of grace. We also speak of being graced by another's presence; the graces of winter reach into all our lives as we and our society are changed by contact with the old. On another level, grace is the entry of God into human life, the unmerited love and favor God shows us. The graces of winter are not simply a matter of trying harder; they are divine gifts, and these gifts are always somehow transforming. They appear in the shape of the grace of Christ, as gifts of life emerging from a struggle with the forces of death. (5)

We understand the meaning of winter grace best when we see it embodied in the lives of older individuals. (5-6)

A spirituality of aging has importance not simply for the old. It may, in fact, be even more necessary for the young. Now that we have come to view the spiritual life not as a static state of the soul, but as movement, growth, and process, the end of the journey becomes an even more decisive influence on every stage. Like the headlight of a train moving swiftly through the night, the later years throw light on the turns and landscapes that lie ahead, preparing us for each passage. (12-13)

If we see in the old only the destruction and loss of all we have known, then we will cling to our present experiences, stunting their growth by our sense that they hold no future promise. (13)

We cannot understand any season of life unless we meditate on all of them. Spring, summer, fall, and winter stand in contrast, but in continuity. Through each of them we learn something of what it means to trust God, to love ourselves, and to love other people. What is planted in one season may not bear fruit until another; what dies in one season may emerge as the beauty of the next. (13)

Having lived through all of the seasons, older persons have a unique sense of the entire life cycle. We have become intensely aware today how interrelated our lives are in terms of space. Communication links us instantly to events around the globe, and we feel their repercussions in every corner of the world. We are just as intertwined in terms of time, though this is less clear today when there is a growing segregation of different age groups in society. How any age-group, young, middle-aged, or old, faces its peculiar challenges affects all other generations. The young create hope or despair in the old; the old do the same for the young. (13)

Winter grace is not simply for those who have reached their later years. Older men and women can be channels of grace and truth for all those about them. The meaning of Christian discipleship comes clear only in the following of Jesus. From the perspective of faith, the later years provide the most intense and vivid revelation of the paradox at the heart of the Christian gospel: that in losing our lives we somehow find them, that loss can be gain, and weakness, strength; that death is the path of life. (15)

To be a human being is to exist between birth and death, to be capable of both wrenching anguish and deep joy. (15)

The Eucharist catches up in symbol this heart of the mystery of the human. In bread and wine it celebrates both the sacred joy of human life and the bitterness of death. In the Eucharist, bread that is blessed and broken becomes food for the world. Those who live to old age know the levels of brokenness that aging brings as well as the blessings of a long life. They can deeply understand the Eucharist and are ready to be both challenged and consoled by it. Perhaps one of the gifts of the later years is to be Eucharist to others, to nourish others from the riches of one's personal experience of brokenness and blessing. (16)

SMALL GROUP DISCUSSION

PARTICIPANTS

people in the Like It or Not transition, along with supportive family members and/or friends

FORMAT

3 sessions of 60 minutes each; initially led by a person skilled in working with the frail elderly (ex: hospice or social worker)

OBJECTIVES

- To support the person during the transition into frailty
- To delineate the roles and responsibilities of the person in transition and family members and/or friends
- To avoid anything that might interfere with the best possible care for the person in transition

MATERIALS

- newsprint
- markers
- copies of Fischer's article

PREPARATION

1. Distribute copies of the Fischer article to the participants.
2. Record on newsprint the guidelines below for good group dynamics.

Instructions

Facilitate good group dynamics by leading participants to observe the following guidelines:

- *Maintain the confidentiality of information shared in the group.* This does not preclude a private conversation between participants who want to work out an issue between themselves that has surfaced in the group meeting. For example, siblings might work out some old jealousies that were aired in the group, and simply bring back to the group news of their reconciliation and their common commitment to the person in transition.
- *Use the "I" perspective when expressing opinions.* For example, if a person in transition into frailty says that she is unsure about God's presence in her life, no one is allowed to say, "You should believe the Bible's promise to us that we are always loved by God." A person could say, however, "I believe that God is with us even in our darkest days," but not as a response to another person's expression of doubt.
- *Give priority to attendance and time constraints.*

Teaching: A Pathway for Spiritual Growth

READING

Balfour Mount is a surgical oncologist now involved in the care of the terminally ill. His book is a poetic reflection written in response to his dying mother's request: "Bal, I have more questions than answers. I thought I had faith. Now I'm not sure. I wish I had something to read." From a deeply held Christian faith, the author writes free verse with titles such as: on learning to trust, finding meaning, promises kept, prayer, freedom, final gift, and silent voice.

Let me find meaning Lord. When faced with finality
                              caught in the crucible!
"It is when we are down and experiencing a time of
adversity that we may be most able to open the doors of our
personalities and expose our needs." (37-38)

No time for pretense.
Masks stripped away.
In the hard light of finality, so much that was treasured
        fades away things,
                events—in the perspective of
                        this light they are
                                but dust.
Instead—
    time
    feelings
    relationships
    to relate to others.
    To give-and in so doing to receive.
    To become empty, by opening, so that we may be filled.
    To recognize that only in dying can we find life
                —dying to ourselves
                —that we may be open to the other. (38)

"Please give her a message," the caller said.
Tell her Miss Brown cannot come today.
But in our place we send a gift.
Give her Isaiah 30:15!
Miss Vallor listened with great intent.
With trace of smile she quietly explained,
"My friend Miss Brown is filled with grace."
I mark her words with utmost care.
Fifty years are gone
since first she led me in his path.
The thought that comes from her today
Must be reflected on.
    —"In quietness and confidence
    Shall be your strength."

I took her hand.
She settled in a drifting sleep.
Minutes passed. I rose to go.
In radiance, she smiled and looked into my eyes.
"It was wonderful," she said. (69)
"Just now, I was with Jesus.
He was sitting on a hill.
Small children were around him.
There were flowers everywhere."
Her lips were dry.
Her limbs were cold
But her eyes, they softly shone
With a sparkling inner light.
Once more she slept.
Again I stirred to leave. Her eyes opened.
"This time I saw him fishing with his men.
They were on the sea
          —And I was there." (70)

Did you see it? God's sign.
Others went to work today,
Their world continuing.
Ours has stopped.
You there, sorrowing her loss, did you see it?
Did you understand?
You who knew her not, standing on the street corner
On your way to work.
Did you see it?
Comprehend?
The winds of God blew through this town today
A mighty wind from a brilliant, cloudless sky.
No storm. No barometric excuse. No thermal alteration.
Just the mighty wind.
                    Spirit with us.
                              His healing presence.

Hour after hour it came. Cleansing all
Touching all you loved, Mother.
Surrounding us—fulfilling his command.
Passing through us
Uplifting. (109-110)

GUIDED MEDITATION
PARTICIPANTS
>   members of the congregation who have experienced a loss during
>   the year

FORMAT
>   3 sessions of 45-60 minutes each; ideally offered during the 3
>   weeks prior to Advent and the first week of the new liturgical year

OBJECTIVES
>   • To acknowledge and name the grief that has accompanied par-
>   ticipants through the current year
>   • To introduce participants to contemplative prayer
>   • To deepen participants' relationship with God through prayer in
>   preparation for the beginning of a new year

PREPARATION
>   1. Divide the Mount article into the following sections: pp. 37-
>   38, pp. 69-70, pp. 109-110.
>   2. Distribute the Mount article to participants.
>   3. Prepare a room setting with comfortable chairs and incandes-
>   cent lighting, perhaps the church parlor.

INSTRUCTIONS
Week 1
>   1. Read aloud the first section of poetry. Allow the participants
>   time to contemplate what has been read. Read the poetry again.
>   (10-15 minutes)
>   2. Invite the participants to a time of silent meditation: Recall the
>   relationship with your loved one who has died. Recall what the
>   person looked like. Think of times in that relationship when

you gave and when you received. Remember how that made you feel. (20 minutes)

3. Begin the closing prayer by reciting the new commandment from Jesus in John 13:34, "I give you a new commandment, that you love one another. Just as I have loved you, you also should love one another." Invite the participants to say the name of the person they remembered during the silent time. End by asking for God's blessing. (10-15 minutes)

4. Invite the participants to share what they experienced during the time of silence. Reinforce the idea that what is said should be held in confidence within the group. (10 minutes)

Week 2

1. Read aloud the first section of poetry. Allow participants time to contemplate what has been read. Read the poetry again. (10-15 minutes)

2. Repeat the portion of Isaiah 30:15 that is in the poetry: "In quietness and confidence shall be your strength." Invite the participants to a time of silent meditation. Ask them to recall a time of sitting in quietness and confidence with the loved one who has died. Ask the following questions: What were your thoughts then? Where was God in those thoughts? Would you put God in the same place now? (20 minutes)

3. Close with this prayer: "The Lord God said, 'In returning and rest you shall be saved; in quietness and in trust shall be your strength.' O Holy One, grant us all rest, quietness, and trust. Amen." (10-15 minutes)

4. Invite the participants to share what they experienced during the time of silence. Reinforce the idea that what is said should be held in confidence within the group. (10 minutes)

Week 3

1. Read aloud the first section of poetry. Allow participants time to contemplate what has been read. Read the poetry again. (10-15 minutes)

2. Invite the participants to a time of silent meditation. Ask them to imagine: the winds of God blowing through you, what the healing presence of God's Spirit can/might feel like, standing on the street corner when God's Spirit swirls around you, being taken away by this wind wherever the Spirit leads you. (20 minutes)

3. Close with this prayer: "Come Holy Spirit. Fall afresh on us. Amen."

4. Invite the participants to share what they experienced during the time of silence. Reinforce the idea that what is said should be held in confidence within the group. (10 minutes)

Prayer: A Pathway to Spiritual Growth

READING

Henry Simmons continues his examination of what various traditions say to people with Alzheimer's Disease and other forms of dementia. He strikes a balance between a "spiritualizing" of the dimming of consciousness and a despair that this dimming of consciousness makes no sense from a faith perspective. This selection turns to a tradition of prayer found in some Christian mystics.

In Western Christianity there is a common wisdom that in the spiritual life purgation precedes illumination and union. There is also a literature of mysticism that speaks of the dark night of the senses and the dark night of the soul: the first a purgation for the spiritually immature, the latter a step towards union. (1)

The darkening of the senses, a physical metaphor for physical frailty . . . the dark night of the senses. It was not about the physical darkening of the sense that John of the Cross was speaking, but there are powerful and instructive parallels worthy of exploration. For John of the Cross, anger, avarice, sloth, lust, pride, gluttony, spiritual envy give way through this night. "At the time of the aridities of this sensory night, God [withdraws] the soul from the life of the senses and [places] it in that of the spirit . . . . Accordingly, people should not mind if the operation of their faculties is being lost to them; they should desire rather that this be done quickly so that they themselves may be no obstacle to the operations of the infused contemplation that God is bestowing . . . " (5)

The darkening of the spirit, a physical metaphor for social isolation and mental frailty [. . .] is the dark night of the spirit. Here the parallels are stunning: "Wishing to strip them of this old [person] and clothe them with the new . . . God divests the faculties, affection, and sense, both spiritual and sensory, interior and exterior. He leaves the intellect in darkness, the will in aridity, the memory in emptiness, and the affections in supreme affliction, bitterness, and anguish, by depriving the soul of the feeling and satisfaction it previously obtained from spiritual blessings. For this privation is one of the conditions required that the spiritual form, which is the union of love, may be introduced into the spirit and united with it. The Lord works all of this in the soul by means of a pure and dark contemplation [. . .]." (5)

Leaving the soul thus empty and dark [. . .] when this spiritual light finds an object on which to shine, that is [. . .] about a judgment on the truth or falsity of some matter, individuals will understand more easily than they did before they were in this darkness. And easily recognizing the imperfection that presents itself, they grow conscious of the spiritual light they possess." (5)

> One dark night
> Fired with love's urgent longings
> —Ah, the sheer grace!—
> I went out unseen,
> My house being now all stilled. (5)

I have no intention of celebrating the dimming of consciousness. Yet we do not know—even in great mental darkening—what is happening in the depths of consciousness. Nor do we know with adequate precision how to describe a self which has transcended the self. These are mysteries and the images of John of the Cross may help us wonder again. (11)

From these strands we may begin to fashion a possible spirituality of frail old age that offers promise and is connected to the wisdom of a powerful (if neglected) part of the spiritual tradition. (11)

GROUP DISCUSSION

PARTICIPANTS

3-4 people in the Like It or Not phase who have recently experienced diminished mental capacities

FORMAT

60 minutes

OBJECTIVES

- To name frailties that the participants are experiencing
- To challenge the participants to find positive aspects of their frailties

MATERIALS

- newsprint
- markers

INSTRUCTIONS

1. Ask the participants to name examples of physical and mental frailties they have experienced. List these in columns on newsprint. If necessary, give some examples to get them started, for example, difficulty remembering names and faces or not being able to hear well. (15 minutes)

2. Now that the frailties are listed for all to see, work with the sense of darkness and light. Ask the participants to determine whether the frailties listed connote light or darkness for them. Have them elaborate on their choice as much as they can. Based on their responses, judge which is considered good—darkness or light—and which is considered bad. Tell the group your conclusion based on what you have heard and see if they agree with you. (20 minutes)

3. Ask the participants to determine if they can see their frailties positively. Can light come from the darkness? This question, of course, assumes that they viewed light positively and darkness negatively. Challenge the group to see a way that God may be working in the frailties many are experiencing to create a spirituality of old age that is unique and distinct. (20 minutes)

4. Close with a time of silent prayer so that the participants may reflect on light, darkness, and the "new" spirituality they may have discovered in this exercise. (5 minutes)

Community: A Pathway for Spiritual Growth

READING

In 1977 Elbert Cole's wife, Virginia, was diagnosed with a condition presumed to be Alzheimer's Disease. She lived for 17 years from the time of diagnosis. The following article is based on an interview that Edward Ansello and Henry Simmons had with Dr. Cole, a Methodist minister and the founder of Shepherd's Centers International.

Virginia has now died. How would you summarize what you learned in giving care?

Self-esteem, dignity, self-respect, safety of self and society, as much independence as possible, beauty, tenderness, stimulation of mind and spirit, patience, discovery, and kindness—all of these had been and now were to continue to be a part of Virginia's life. This was the guiding principle for the specifics of caregiving and management. (1)

What was the first thing you did following Virginia's diagnosis?

The first thing we did was to hold a family conference. We decided that caregiving is a family affair, a partnership that also included some friends. Even though I would be the primary caregiver, I never felt I was alone. If some cultures can talk about a whole village educating a child, it is healthy to think of the whole community having a part in caregiving. We found family conferences very helpful and had them frequently, in person or more often by telephone. (1)

How would you articulate the fundamental principle of caregiving?

Caregiving is a shared experience involving family members and the care recipient. The family divided up responsibilities among all of us. Our daughter in California would take responsibility for clothes selection and personal grooming. Every two months she flew in to our home in Kansas City to do her part. Our son, a scientist, took responsibility to read the research, eagerly hoping for the breakthrough that never came. Virginia was included in all conversations and all decisions. (1)

How did you arrange your life day in and day out?

We decided to commit ourselves to maintaining the same lifestyle as we had lived before the onset of the disease. No one was to deviate from or eliminate duties to "take care of Virginia." Rather we would include her and accommodate any special needs she might develop within our commitments and duties. We included Virginia at every point, allowing her to experience the stimulation of our work and our schedules. (2)

That must have meant some difficulties and risks.

We talked a lot about this stance and viewed it as an important way for her to know she was very much included in everything we did. This meant a busy life, considerable involvement in the community, and the continuation of our heavy schedules. We would be reasonable and use common sense. We lived with risk and accepted its consequences. (2)

So Virginia was very much involved in her own caregiving?

In caregiving we found it important to affirm Virginia as a person. Her blemishes or frailty never outweighed her affirming qualities. Good caregiving is based on equality and partnership. The caregiver is not superior and the care recipient inferior, nor ever made to feel so. (2)

I never apologized for Virginia's incapacities, nor was I ever ashamed of anything she said or did. She smiled at funerals, of which as a clergy wife she attended many. She often inquired about deceased members of a family, not remembering their deaths. She brushed lint off women's or men's suits, and if people talked too loud, she would "shush" them. Her smile was consuming and so very intimate. (2)

Granted, at times this was difficult. Caregivers have some work to do with themselves in mental attitude, spiritual support, and physical renewal. In fact, it is fair to say that good caregiving starts with the caregiver. Society needs to help caregivers take care of themselves. They need to make sure they have access to good resources. (2)

As the disease progressed, what changes did you have to make?

I had to learn to let Virginia express herself as she wanted to and to trust that people would not reject her. For example, Virginia liked to walk through shopping malls. As we walked, she might spot a child and young mother and go right to them, patting the child and stroking the attractive dress of the mother. I would stand 10 or 12 feet away, not wanting to invade what for her must have been a moment of memory. If she lingered without coming back to me, I would quietly join her, smile at her new friends, gently take her arm, and move on. (2)

Toileting became the real challenge, and I had assumed ultimate failure to handle that department would require a major shift in our caregiving. We practiced the simple rule of providing her an opportunity for voiding every 2 hours. The rule is simple, but trying to find the place is complicated. (If people can make a fortune publishing lists of the best restaurants, we should do well with a book on the best toilets of America.) (2)

Amazingly she remained continent for the entire 17 years except during the nights of the last year. (2)

Seventeen years is an extraordinarily long time for caregiving. Was communication burdensome?

For 16 of the 17 years we interacted as persons in love, although our ways of interacting changed. Even though Virginia could not follow conversations, the words flowed through her, and she seemed to feel included. I realized Virginia was in every way a real person with all of the needs of a real person. Her limitation was her loss of connecting thought and meaning, her cognitive capacity. Hand-holding came naturally, and we had our way of three squeezes to suggest either "I love you" or "I want you." (3)

So continued interaction was the key to maintaining your quality of life?

We wanted Virginia to live with dignity, maximize her independence, engage daily in stimulating experiences, and discover joy and pleasure along the way. I could only imagine what it would feel like to live in a foggy darkness of a disconnected world. We "majored" in stimulation rather than follow sedentary patterns, and I sincerely believe it made caregiving easier. (3)

All this must have tried Virginia's faith and trust in God?

Virginia, like most persons, had spiritual needs. Her simple and uncomplicated faith from the days of our courtship had been a trademark of her life. For a period of time she dressed herself each day and would say, "We are going to be late for church." Every day seemed to be Sunday . . . not really a bad blemish. At church she enjoyed the children, our friends, the organ, and the singing. Much of the service she ignored, but would noticeably come alive when something connected. (3)

And she was able to maintain her trust and faith?

Virginia's faith continued to nurture her even as her limitations progressed. As I tucked her in for the night, a couple of hours before I retired, I would alternate reciting the Lord's Prayer or the 23rd Psalm, and give her a kiss. She, to the end, would look up at me with a smile and then tweak her nose as a sign of absolute security and love. (3)

At many levels, this caregiving seems heroic. Was it that for you?

No. No big deal, no unbearable burden. Just a family and friends providing a little extra help to Virginia, so she could enjoy a moment here or there and know she was loved. (3)

TRAINING FOR MINISTRY PROJECT

PARTICIPANTS

congregants who are experiencing dementia; their volunteer aids

FORMAT

60 minutes

OBJECTIVE·

• To identify and train congregants who will "stand alongside" (in every sense) those in the congregation who grow frail, physically or mentally

INSTRUCTIONS

Enlist a nurse to train volunteers who will "provide a little extra help" as needed, according to the model used by Elbert Cole. Of course, this help should never be given without asking, "May I sit with you?" or, "Would you like me to be with you to give you a hand should you need it?" or, "I would like to sit with you. May I?"

Witness: A Pathway for Spiritual Growth

READING

Brynolf Lyon explores the relationship of human fulfillment and aging. This relationship is foundational to pastoral care with older adults. The author critically probes the claims of historic theological literature on older adulthood along with contemporary theological interpretations of experience. Out of these he produces a "practical theology" of old age.

The peculiarity for us today of the claim that fulfillment in aging is marked by growth lies in two directions. First, it may seem trite or simply obvious that *fulfillment* at whatever stage of life is a matter of growth and not decline. The piety of self-actualization in our time is such that "growth" appears the *sine qua non* of the most desirable way of life. [. . .] However fully we may have granted the difficulty of making adequate sense of the idea of growth with respect to most life periods, though, aging is still seriously susceptible to the sentimentalizing and romanticizing of "growth." (55)

Perhaps this is a reaction to the second peculiarity of the idea of growth with aging: aging and *decline* seem such a natural pair. [. . .] The association of aging with decline and loss in our experience is frequently so powerful that we seem to be left with either simply rejecting the idea of growth with aging altogether or romanticizing it to avoid the seemingly too painful realities. (55-56)

God's actions of blessing are but one dimension of the way in which Christians have sought to describe the horizon of human experience. It is a way in which the horizons of our experience of the cycle of generations and the continuities of our lives are made meaningful: the values that we realize in our everyday lives are enabled by God's actions of blessing. To speak of the blessing of age, therefore, may seem to mean that there is a *characteristic value* that may be realized in later adulthood (which is obviously not to say it is the only value realized in later adulthood). (113)

Herein lies one response to the problem of hope in aging, for God's blessing is understood as God's envisioning of a potential for the realization of the greatest value for each moment and condition of our lives. God's granting of blessing, in this sense, is unconditional: within each moment and condition God's blessing is present. The moment or condition *itself* is not God's blessing, but rather God blesses us in each moment and condition by offering us the possibility of the creation of value. While God's blessing is unconditional, however, the actual realization of value in our lives requires our action. The fruit of God's blessing may be realized or not, may be actively thwarted by us or be but partially realized in our brokenness. Our realizing the fruits of God's blessing in our lives is not the sole action of God, but the co-creating of God and the world. (114)

Two points about this reconceptualization need to be highlighted. First, the blessing of age here is understood as unconditional in the sense that God's actions of blessing are not withheld in the face of human brokenness or sin. Such a view seems consistent with the Christian witness. In the Christ-event, we witness to the *universal* love and forgiveness of God. [. . .] Blessing is an aspect of God's pure, unbounded love. While God's granting of blessing is unconditional, our realization of the fruits of God's blessing is hardly guaranteed. God's blessing is not a magic formula uttered from above that guarantees our good fortune. We must recognize, with the process theologians, that God does not (cannot) solely determine the outcome of events in the world. (114)

Real human freedom . . . carries with it real human responsibility. In a world not guaranteed of the emergence of the good by divine fiat, there is the threat of real evil and the consequent necessity of human action toward the realization of the good in our world and in our lives. In more traditional language, God's will is not so much enacted onto recalcitrant history as it is a persuasive force that may yet be modified, thwarted, or positively embodied in our own becoming and the becoming of our world. God's blessing is unconditional, but our realization of the fruits of God's blessing is not. The blessing of age, therefore, is offered by God to each older adult, but its actualization depends on their response to that blessing. (115)

Second, to speak of the blessing of age is not to say that we must see the various conditions that may afflict those in older adulthood as good or, worse, as God's "reward" or (if we think God's blessing is absent) God's "punishment" of us. God's blessing does not refer to God's envisioning a potential in the best of all possible worlds (which is the way many of us are likely to understand it), but rather to God's envisioning a potential in our real world and our present circumstances within it. To speak of the blessing of age, therefore, is not to say that old age is devoid of hardship, loss, or disease. Rather, it is to say that God provides a potential for the realization of the greatest value even in these circumstances. (115)

The idea of the blessing of age here does not require us to romanticize hardship, loss, or disease. . . . But loss is not all there is, even though sometimes it is all we can see. God suffers with us in our hardship, loss, or disease, and offers us blessing. God suffers with the victim of Alzheimer's Disease, with the destitute aged of our great cities. God experiences the pain of an aging self struggling to maintain coherence. God suffers with us and offers us blessing—the power of life in the face of death. God suffers with us and offers us the power of a life-giving self. (115)

In Jesus, God's actions of blessing and redemption are disclosed as integrally related. Through God's redemptive action, the realization of value in our lives is saved from final meaninglessness. In God's redemptive action, God creatively synthesizes all other things into his own actual being as God. God takes in the value realized in the world, weaves it into Godself, and thus preserves it everlastingly—even to the extent of its contributing to the ongoing blessing of God in our lives and the becoming of our world. It is because God redeems our lives from final meaninglessness that the blessing of age carries the force that it does: the question of the meaningfulness of one's moral becoming, and its potential relational resolution, occur in a world where God confirms the seriousness of this venture of the aging self. (116-17)

BIBLE STUDY

TOPIC

"Laughing at the Possibilities"

SCRIPTURE

Genesis 18:1-15

PARTICIPANTS

women's study circle, which in many churches is composed of primarily older women who are in the Like It or Not stage of life

FORMAT

60 minutes

OBJECTIVES

- To connect the story of Abraham and Sarah with Lyon's point that God's blessings are unconditional
- To discover the fruits of God's blessings in the participants' lives
- To turn the participants' discoveries into witness to others

INSTRUCTIONS

1. Read together Genesis 18:1-15 in the manner that best suits your group, either aloud or silently. (10 minutes)
2. Discuss: God gave an unconditional blessing to Abraham and Sarah long after the birth of a son was expected. Did they "deserve" God's unconditional blessing? Recall some of the stories of their lives that are contained in Genesis to answer this question. Given their history together, were Abraham and Sarah able to recognize God's blessings in the past? Ask the participants to be specific in their responses. (15 minutes)
3. Discuss: One of Lyon's main points is that God's blessing is unconditional, but our realization of the fruits of God's blessing is not. How did Sarah react to the conversation she overheard between Abraham and the 3 visitors? Do you think that at least part of Sarah's reaction stemmed from her age? Was Sarah's reaction to be expected given her age? (15 minutes)
4. Discuss: How can we work on recognizing God's blessings? (It may be helpful for the participants to look into their past for

evidence of God's blessings and their reaction to these blessings.) How can we turn our acceptance of God's blessing into a ministry of witness to others? You may wish to make a covenant with one another, pledging to be supportive in this ministry of witness. (15 minutes)

5. Close with prayer that focuses on the ministry of witness to God's unconditional blessings. (5 minutes)

Source Notes

Molly Tully and Joan Turner, *Join the Club: Meeting the Special Needs of Men with Alzheimer's Disease* (Washington: c/o Friends Meeting of Washington, 2111 Florida Avenue NW, Washington DC 20008, 1992). This book is available by calling 1-703-478-3695. The proceeds are donated to the Club.

Kathleen Fischer, *Winter Grace: Spirituality for the Later Years* (New York/Mahwah NJ: Paulist, 1985).

Balfour M. Mount, *Sightings in the Valley of the Shadow* (Chicago: Inter-Varisty, 1983). Used by permission of the author.

Henry C. Simmons, "Visions, Darkness, Light," in *Aging and the Human Spirit 2* (2) (Fall 1992) 4-11.

John of the Cross, "The Dark Night," in *John of the Cross: Selected Writings*, trans. and ed. K. Kavenaught (Mahwah NJ: Paulist, 1987) 184, 186, 199-200, 203-204.

Edward Ansello and Henry Simmons, "Caregiving: Vision, Spirit, and Person," in *The Interfaith Coalition for Older Virginians Link-Letter*, an interview with Dr. Elbert C. Cole 4/1 (Spring 1997). Used by permission of the authors.

K. Brynolf Lyon, *Toward a Practical Theology of Aging* (Philadelphia PA: Fortress, 1985).

chapter 5

THE REST OF LIVING

Witness: A Pathway for Spiritual Growth

READING

According to James L. Empereur, a Roman Catholic, in the liturgical renewal after Vatican Council II, the "sacrament of anointing" replaced Extreme Unction—a sacrament for the dying. Currently in their books of common worship, many Protestant churches include an anointing of the sick. The Church of the Brethren, which has always had an anointing of the sick, offers an understanding of anointing that captures its meaning for all traditions. Anointing connects with people at various crisis points in their lives and is offered for the forgiveness of sin, the strengthening of faith, and healing and wholeness according to God's will.

The sacrament of anointing when administered to the elderly brings to expression significant elements in the Christian perspective on human life:

- That old age has its own merits, beauty, and worth; and it must not be marginalized by contemporary society.
- That reconciliation in the Church includes the acceptance of one's total humanity. This demands reconciliation not only with those who are actually in old age, but reconciliation with one's aging self.
- That the world's criterion for evaluating the worth of the person needs to be revised.

It is not what you do but who you are that counts. The anointing of the elderly should be the liturgical climax of the community's care and love of these people. The celebration must be based upon attempts to integrate them fully as members of the Christian Church. But anointing the elderly says more. It proclaims to all in the Church that life is a continual progress of growth, that each stage of life must be accepted if life is to be lived abundantly. (13)

Although during the time of old age there are increasing forms of disengagement from what constituted the source of value in human living, a need to achieve a sense of continuity must be recognized. Even the very elderly must be able to feel that they are caring for others in some way, that even in their old age there is usefulness. The sacrament of anointing can point to the importance of transcending individual life cycles. This is done through care which has lasting significance. It is the sacrament of anointing which can articulate the hope that one's caring efforts are caught up in the activity of God and so transcend their human origin. Christian anointing speaking of salvation means that human values are preserved in God. One need not sink back into a dysfunctional self-preservation but can have hope since renewal of the world is not dependent on one's activities alone. One's caring efforts will go beyond one's labors. What any individual has done has been taken up into God and has become a participant in God's continual urging of the world to renewal. (163)

The special vocation in the Church which belongs to the elderly is not an easy one. These people must also be courageous witnesses. No longer spurred on by the enthusiasm of youth or the expectancy of the inexperienced, these elderly have been sobered through the years by their own limitations and failures. What precisely can they offer the young for whom success is seemingly near at hand and for whom all is still possible? The message appears to be one of sadness more than hope. (169)

What they articulate, what their lives are living paradigms of is that *life is worthwhile*, life is worth closing well not because of what has been achieved by an individual, but because one's very being is of *worth*. It is the often quoted but little accepted dictum that it is not what you do but what you are that is of ultimate significance. Anointing can put in a Christian perspective that the value of old age springs from the meaning of life itself. It can bring to ritual expression the faith one can have in life. (169-70)

The sacrament of anointing should proclaim clearly that the meaning of old age is that life is worth closing well, just as any other part of life is worth living well. To grow old, then, is to believe in the worth of one's life. But this is not an easy task. Courage is the desired virtue for the elderly, and only a courageous faith can deal with the sense of loss and diminishment, the lack of self-esteem, the suppressed guilt and feeling of abandonment which are the temptations at this time of life. Anointing is the celebration that in Christ and his Church one need not let such experiences control one's life. Through anointing, the community visits elderly persons to assure them of the power of old age. Liturgically, the Church is saying that it needs these old people if the incarnation is to make sense on the human level. (172)

For the elderly, anointing can assure them that in their weakness they can find their strength. They can now accept each moment of their lives as gift. They need no longer try to control the lives of others. They can be free from the expectations to fulfill certain societal roles. No longer is there any imperative to spend time and energy on plans for a better tomorrow. They are achieving their purposes; they are fulfilling their vocation by being old and by being old in a Christian integral way. Old people have less time but more space. They can now explore the space of their inner worlds. (174)

Resignation is one of the required and hoped-for virtues of this time of life. But such resignation must be more than mere passivity in the face of physical and moral evil. The attitude which calls for a "giving up and letting all in God's hands" may turn out to be another form of cowardice. The sacrament of anointing calls the elderly to move beyond this kind of misguided "virtue." God is not simply present in human passivities, but where people choose to grow in the face of opposition. There is no time in one's declining years when the human growth process is at an end. Christian resignation means accepting one's life as it is in faith and struggling with that life so that any given moment is not absolutized or, perhaps better put, "finalized." There is always a future. There is always a movement. (175)

One of the major ways in which anointing the elderly challenges the Church, and these old people thereby exercise their ministry to the Church at large, is the way in which they call into question the culturally accepted values of the worshipers. The fact is that people who are initiated as infants, formed in a family, educated in the school system, and taken into the job status, are not asked to undergo any kind of conversion. (179)

A culture which is money- and success-oriented will find it almost impossible to have much appreciation for old age. The elderly are offensive to such a culture because they contradict its own value system. Thus, along with the poor, American society attempts to hide these people. It is precisely the sacrament of anointing which can call for a conversion of values in this area on the part of Christians. Anointing becomes the symbolic call for depth and spiritual sensibility which are part of the Christian maturing process so that when the time of diminishing powers and dependence on others arrives, these Christians will have learned how to find their significance in that attitude which runs contrary to prevailing cultural perspectives. (179-80)

ANOINTING SERVICE

Participants

elders in The Rest of Living stage

Format

This ritual may take place in a nursing home or in a church. It may be a special service or part of a Sunday service or part of a service dedicated to the wholeness of a congregation. When used in this manner, emphasis is placed on the witness that anointing of older adults can make in a congregation. This ritual may take place during a week or month that recognizes older adults. (Handwashing/footwashing may be substituted for anointing if that is more in keeping with denominational tradition.)

OBJECTIVES
- To affirm that old age has its merits, beauty, and worth
- To assure the elderly that they are valuable in God's eyes

MATERIALS
- oil for anointing
- bowl of water, drying cloth*

(*If hand/footwashing is used)

PREPARATION

Set up the worship space with the materials needed for the ritual.

INSTRUCTIONS

Follow this service outline: (30-45 minutes)

- *Opening Sentences*—Read a Scripture having to do with whole-ness (ex: Isa 40:31).
- *Prayer of Confession*—This prayer could be corporate, including the challenges that aging presents to our culture and to our church communities (as Empereur highlights in the article). The prayer could end uplifting the significant elements in the Christian perspective on human life that anointing can express (see the first paragraph of the Empereur article).
- *Declaration of Forgiveness*—A statement that assures those gathered that they are forgiven through Jesus Christ
- *Scripture*—Psalm 121
- *Ritual*—Introduce anointing as a way of recognizing the value of life as a gift from God and as a way of expressing the love and care that the community feels for the older adults who will be anointed. Set apart those who will be anointed. (Ex: They could be seated together, or you could ask them to come forward or be brought forward.) If the congregation is to also lay on hands, invite them to do so at this time. As each person is anointed, say his or her name, and make the sign of the cross on his or her forehead with oil on your finger and say, "I anoint you with oil in the name of the Father, and of the Son, and of the Holy Spirit." You may include a short prayer thanking God for the life of the person.

- *Concluding Prayer*—Offer a final prayer of thanksgiving, leaving time for those who wish to offer their own prayers, either silently or aloud.
- *Benediction*—"Go in peace."

Service: A Pathway to Spiritual Growth

READING

Translated from French, the series of brief meditations from which this selection is taken is so specific to the life and culture of its author, Joseph Folliet, that the reader gets a glimpse of the way age and culture are intertwined. His book could serve as a model of writing a journal that reflects finely honed, mature wisdom. It is straightforward, lucid, and inspiring. Although we know the date of publication of the English translation (1983), we do not know the date of publication of the original book or the age of the author when he wrote it.

Accepting old age is also accepting loneliness or dependence or both together, because we can be very lonely when we are most cared for by others. However surrounded we are by loving people, we are alone, for those of our own generation, with whom we can speak as equals and exchange mutual reminiscences, become fewer each day. And those who love and care for us are aware of our weakness and are anxious about us, so they surround us with precautions that keep us in a state of dependence. Little children depend on women—usually their mothers, of course—and so do old people—they depend on female relatives, nurses, and nuns. (52)

An acceptance of one's dependence may, however, be a cause of joy. It will prove that those near to us love us, even though they love us clumsily and leave us little freedom. It will remind us of human solidarity and the love of God that is grafted on to that solidarity. For our part, we can react to those loving attentions that keep us prisoner by little acts that show that we are still free. We can, for example, smile, make a joke, give a present, or do a kindness. People gossiped, complained, and quarreled in the big working-class homes of an earlier generation, but there was also a tremendous solidarity. It was not emphasized or expressed orally, but it existed. The middle-aged mother, for example, did shopping and small tasks for the grandfathers and grandmothers and sometimes even all their housework. In return, the old ones looked after the kids. This is not a fairy story—it is what happened when I was young. There is nothing humiliating in being dependent. We simply have to accept it. It is natural. (53)

In my mind's eye I can still see my grandfather sitting in the evening sun smoking, in the garden which he cultivated with such love. He smoked a carefully seasoned clay pipe—one of those pipes costing 2 or 3 pence in those days, no longer obtainable now, but then very well suited to the less-than-modest resources of those who smoked them. Sucking at his pipe, he would proudly contemplate his vegetables and flowers. He did not speak much and loved to be alone, sunk in thought. What were his thoughts? I never knew, and it is quite likely that he did not either. But his relaxed face showed that his soul was at peace. When I joined my childish thoughts to his old man's meditation, I was always careful not to disturb him. He did not stop gardening, smoking his pipe, and dreaming until he was 77, when he was struck down by a heart attack, like an oak tree struck by lightning. In fact, his solid, heavy body always reminded me of an oak tree, so perhaps his end was the right one. (57)

I can already hear several old people complaining: I would love to serve others, and I suffer continuously because I feel so useless. But whom can I serve? And in what way? I have often offered, but no one wants my services. I have been thrown on the rubbish heap. There is a great deal of truth in this objection. Many younger people regard the aged *a priori* as worn out and useless and think that it might be wrong to throw them in the dustbin, but that their real place is the junk cupboard, together with chipped china or the junk room with its old boxes and trunks full of all kinds of odds and ends. At the same time, I think my dear old friends who complain in this way ought to examine their consciences. (109)

Have you, in offering your services, not wanted perhaps to dominate others? Perhaps you were hardly conscious of this—maybe quite unconscious. Did you not want to impose yourself on others or at least impose some of your views on them? I am thinking especially of the relationships between elderly parents and their offspring with young families. And old, experienced workers with long service in an organization that has changed—not only its staff, but also its methods and even its aims. The old person ought to serve humbly—and humility is a gratuitous form of service. I know how hard that can be, but I think it is best to resign oneself to it. Perhaps you should not just wait for invitations and congratulations to come to you. You might try asking people to let you serve them in ways that they want. And don't take offence! However strange it may seem and however much men [sic] may need each other, it is never easy to serve others. You have to be recognized and accepted as a servant. Jesus understood this—he came, not to be served, but to serve. (110)

Despite all these difficulties, I still believe that the old person has a part to play in society. The old person is no longer now what that person was in the past, in a traditional agricultural society, nor is that person the same as in the previous century, which was a time of transition. But he does seem to be as necessary as he always was. Or as she always was. (110)

It is not a new idea in spiritual writing to compare life with a pilgrimage. It is as old as spiritual literature itself, but its age does not make it any less relevant to us today. Humans are essentially travelers through time. The Christian sees this journey as a pilgrimage, a continuous journey toward a divine end. The whole of humankind is going on a pilgrimage through time, passing on its way through many cities and civilizations. (173)

One of the great Christian paradoxes is that those who till the soil and build cities must go on planting and building as though they were to be settled forever, yet at the same time always be conscious that the individual and the world that person creates are passing. We are pilgrims with no permanent dwelling place, and the human condition is that of a traveler. (173)

We are most sharply aware of this apparent contradiction when we are old. We old people have not in any sense finished our work. We go on planting and building to provide food and shelter for those who follow us. But we feel that our time is limited and that our work is always exposed to chance. This is, I think, why so many old people go about things with such feverish haste. They have to finish what they are doing while the light of day is still there for them and while they still have the strength to go forward and to create. I do not think they are behaving very wisely. True wisdom consists in doing what we have to do calmly, without restlessness and excitement, and leaving to God the cares of tomorrow that we cannot deal with today. Let us, then, continue on our pilgrimage, putting one foot in front of the other, until we reach the last inn—the inn of death, which is also a chapel. (174)

Let us continue to climb as long as the evening sun is shining. We can always stop from time to time, get our breath back, and rest our tired old legs. But God is calling us from the heights and will not let us sit down for long. And God certainly will not let us go down again! The pilgrimage is not over yet—let us be on our way! In front of us there is Christ, carrying the cross and showing us the way. And at the very top the Easter light of the Resurrection is shining. Let us go up in the evening sun. (175)

GROUP REFLECTION

PARTICIPANTS
    a men's class that has a number of members who are beginning to grow frail as well as some who are still in good health

FORMAT
    60 minutes

OBJECTIVE
    • To give to God the concerns that the participants are unable to effect so that they can let go and experience God in a different way

MATERIALS
    • copies of Folliet's reflections (lg. print)
    • copies of the poem "O Spirit of Love" (lg. print)
    • pencils or pens
    • a candle
    • matches

PREPARATION
    Arrange the room in a relaxed, well-lit, comfortable manner.

INSTRUCTIONS
    1. Distribute copies of the Folliet article and pencils or pen. Ask the
       participants to read Folliet's reflections silently and to underline a
       phrase or sentence that strikes them as important. When all have
       finished reading, ask the participants to read slowly and without
       commentary the words that were underlined. (20 minutes)
    2. Discuss the Folliet article paragraph by paragraph. Read the
       opening sentence of each paragraph and then ask for discus-
       sion. (35 minutes)
    3. Distribute copies of the poem. Ask the participants to sit in
       silence for a moment. Light the candle, and place it in the mid-
       dle of the group. Then read the poem, slowly and reflectively,
       or read it responsively. (5 minutes)

O Spirit of Love

O Holy Spirit, Spirit of love,
tireless giver living in our souls in order to make us conform to
    the Man-God
and to bring us as adopted children to God's glorious love,
I stretch out my old, clumsy hands to you.
Pour into them the treasure of your gifts.

In my youth, you gave me the gift of strength.
"I am writing to you, young men, because you are strong," the
    old man, Saint John, said.
With your strength, I have fought against giants and demons,
I have crossed rivers and seas and have climbed mountains.
I have experienced victory and defeat in turn.
But with your strength I have also stood up after every fall.
And I have gone on fighting.

In my mature years, you gave me the gift of knowledge.
Through you, I plunged down into the abyss and entered the
    infinite space of heaven.
Through you, I learned the secrets of nature and the human
    heart.
Through you, I perceived the depths of the deity.
Through you, I was thrilled with the joy of knowledge.
O Holy Spirit, in my old age, give me the gift of wisdom and
    benevolence, wisdom's companion.
Through you, let me taste the fruit of the tree of life and enable
    others to taste it.
Through you, let me no longer be surprised by anything, but let
    me go on admiring.

Let me not try to be understood, but to understand.
Let my words be distilled and made into the pure golden liquid
    of living truth.
Let me always forgive others infinitely and not demand
    forgiveness from them—let me be satisfied with your
    forgiveness.
Let me give counsel and respect my brothers' freedom.
Let me live fully in the present and only look forward to
    eternity.

O Holy Spirit, may your dew and your fire rain on my old
    heart,
so that it is full of that love
which is the only true wisdom. Amen. (132-33)

Proclamation: A Pathway for Spiritual Growth

READING

John LaFarge, writing in his 80s, begins with the assumption that "old age has its own meaning, like any other phase of human life, and that the wisest thing to do, when old age has crept up on us, would be to explore that meaning and to adopt some general plan of action, so as really to profit from it" (11).

The power of this archetypal principle of growth through diminishment does not arise from some mysterious or mystical excellence which would attach to "diminishment" as such, for what is negative in its nature remains merely negative. Its power relies upon something altogether different; it rests upon the sworn word of the all-powerful Creator, who has given us a hope, a firm and unshaken hope. The strength of old age lies in the firmness of that hope. (33)

So I accept each day as a gift, all my days as a gift, regardless of whether or not they bring me golden bowls. Each day is an opportunity to renew my confidence in the sworn word, the steadfast promises of the Creator. My attitude is not one of querulous questioning as to why I have not more days, but rather complete thanks that I have even another day in which to praise God, to love Him, to serve Him and fulfill His holy will. By the same token, I accept the temporary, limited burden of sorrow, humiliation, and the degree of punishment that accompanies my hope. These humiliating aspects of my human existence, these diminishments of old age, are so bound up with my future hopes that Paradise would be meaningless for me were it not in some way associated with this life's deprivations. Time, each day, each hour, is a gift, because it is in time, and through time's day-to-day vicissitudes, that the Creator works in us and for us the glory of the future life. (43)

The more meaning you have found in life, the clearer will be the meaning of old age. If life were static, if we never changed, if life were like the surface of the moon, we would have antiquity, yes—we would be chronologically old. But we would not grow old in the human sense. (25)

Precisely in these latter days you become aware of a new life growing: with a freshness and vitality beyond the categories of other new experiences. You become aware of something that has been with you, very likely, since childhood—that you have loved and honored, yet comes to you now with new meanings. It speaks to you not of either past or present but of the future; or rather it doesn't speak to you in terms of time at all. Silently, unobtrusively, steadily (unless you deliberately thwart it) a new life grows within you: the presence of Him who is the Resurrection and the Life. It is none other than the birth and growth of divine charity: of love for God and man. (84)

If given any freedom, given its logical course, this new life will invade your old life: will possess you, will *create* a new being within you. In old age, in other words, you become much less a record of what you have once been by your (bygone) efforts, as a record of what the Creator is working out within you: the birth of this new life, the life of the Resurrection, the life of Eternity. . . . For now life has found its *true* meaning. The meaning of age is the meaning of life itself: life as the workshop of the Creator, ever vivifying, perfecting, developing our own true selves within us. (84)

The sign of this divine operation is the presence of charity: love of God and man, love seen as a gift, poured out in our hearts by the Spirit of God. (84)

There is no condition of mind or body, in which I cannot in some way, in some fashion or manner, practice some form of love for God and man. Sickness, suffering, death itself can be offered up as a holocaust of love. At the time of this life's greatest weakness, I have at my disposal the exercise of a social dynamism, which exceeds in the long run any merely human force. I don't say that my individual action will manifest that force: it will pass unnoticed, save for the very few, or the chance individual, who may benefit by it. But it is known to God; it is part of His divine operation on earth, and as such it is part of His all-conquering enterprise. Once we begin to grasp this truth, we are surprised to see what a perspective it opens up to us. (85)

If we are truly grateful for the gift of life, we shall value the gift in new and unexpected ways. For we shall learn that life, as it is given us by the Creator, bears within itself the power of reparation, making amends for its own delinquencies. It has the power, through His grace and mercy, of re-creating itself. The mathematical discovery of relativity can *in theory* enable a person to live a year's time in a single month, if you are traveling at something like 99.5 percent of the speed of light. But relativity cannot mend the past. Reparation is God's gift to us time-bound mortals. We can exercise it each day, each moment, that we simply and honestly thank Him for the mere gift of being alive. (126)

If I have had the courage to accept life and all that the Creator does with me and for me during the course of each day of that life, if I have let Him work with me, let Him have His own peculiar and inexplicable way with me during this pilgrimage, I shall not be hopelessly perplexed when I come to the end of this term. The Amen of death will be simply the logical successor of all the Amens I have spoken throughout my entire life: Amens that I have spoken, because of my Creator's Amen in heaven, Amens that mean I am trying to walk with God. (129-30)

SERMON
TOPIC
"Genuine Love"

SCRIPTURE
John 13:31-35

FOCUS
Old age can bring new life with the growing awareness of God's presence that is expressed as greater love of neighbor.

FUNCTION
Given that many older people feel diminished physically, emotionally, and spiritually, they may not recognize the gift they have within themselves to share God's love with the world.

THEME

There are many members of the church who no longer worship with us because they are frail. We, too, will someday be in that time of life. Let us take time, in remembering them, to reflect on the meaning of old age and on what it takes to age with grace. Growing old requires courage to live and to accept what natural life brings. Aging also requires courage to live so that the divine within us may be manifested as love for our neighbor. The courage to live in this manner springs from the firmness of hope that results from the promises God has made and God's steadfastness to those promises throughout the years. Older adults have the power to share God's love in the way that Jesus showed God's love. This love has the power to bring new meaning to life in the later years.

Teaching: A Pathway for Spiritual Growth

READING

In this selection Henry Simmons and Mark Peters write for people who want to engage in pastoral visitation in nursing homes, but who do not have a clear idea of what is involved. They describe nursing homes past and present and offer a plan of visitation that minimizes discomfort and maximizes pastoral effectiveness.

A study of the perception of needs in three long-term care facilities compares the residents' understanding of their needs for pastoral care and that of their pastors. The residents said unanimously that what helped them move through impact and recoil to reorganization and adaptation was personal prayer. The pastoral ministers, on the other hand, thought the need was for communal worship, for collective activities. While both ministers and residents agreed on the need for reassurance, for the re-creation of a meaningful life, and for a personal relationship with God, the residents reported that these needs were met through private and personal spiritual activity and deeper involvement in the internal side of spirituality. (96)

The pastoral question, then, is what we can do to help people develop the inner side of their lives of devotion. Or, more simply, what is it that we can do to help new residents in nursing homes to pray? Before addressing the specifics of engaging in this pastoral task, it is well noted that we may approach this task with a sense of unease, even of dread. Why? To come close to the inner life of another in such a moment of darkness puts to the test the adequacy of our meditation on the mysteries of faith, puts to the test whether our own psyche and souls are refined by fire, puts to the test the quality of our own inner lives. What is needed by the new resident is a guide whose specific qualifications are rooted in a serious struggle with the same ultimate realities and some sureness of knowledge about the inner life of prayer. (97)

What can you do to help people pray at this specific moment of pastoral need? First, we can understand the importance of personal prayer and the inner life for assurance, for the re-creation of a meaningful life, and for a new relationship with God. (Concomitantly we must recognize that communal activities are *not* what is needed.) If we truly understand this, at least the new resident does not have to apologize for what is happening or for the chosen path for resolution. (97)

Second, we can help by understanding what a difficult task is the re-creation of meaning. Neither the culture nor the church culture has an adequate sense of what it means to grow old. To make sense of old age, frailty, sickness, homelessness, and death is an unenviable burden. (97)

Third, we can help unlink personal prayer and worship, not simply by stepping back from the conviction that what is needed at this moment is collective worship, but by actively addressing the issue. Although this may seem to run contrary to the thrust of this book, it highlights how specific is this moment in the life of a nursing home resident, and how personal is the struggle to make a successful transition. People will say that they have prayed personal prayers, but in some measure their prayers have been supported by familiar people, familiar places, and familiar weekly rhythms of prayer. Now the places the resident prayed are no longer their places of prayer; and the self who prayed there is no longer the same self. The resident cannot go home again, physically or spiritually. There is a sense of uprootedness that needs to be articulated forthrightly. Only when it is named is it fair to add that it is possible to begin to pray again in this new old age. (97-98)

Fourth, with those for whom these are issues, we must be able to contend with and to deal with the anger and the frustration toward God that may be part of the transition. Anger toward God is not a fashionable topic for sermons. But at this stage there will be a profound sense of disappointment in God, and for some a profound sense that life (that is, God and family) has cheated them. For others the emotion will be anger and then desolation—a sense that there is no consolation in God. (98)

The classics of the spiritual life speak about the dark night of the senses and of the soul. One of the reasons we lift up minds and hearts to God is that we find certain consolation in it—a certain quietness, a certain wellness. The expectation that this is a legitimate outcome of prayer is fostered by a common assumption that prayer has something to do with feeling well about ourselves, so that we are not burdened by desolation, by no sense of center, by no sense of connectedness, by no sense of the mystery of the presence of God. (98)

In the face of moments of desolation, whenever the courage to will God's will seems repugnant, we need to approach our parishioner with understanding so that there will be no appeal to the old ways. People who are experiencing desolation in prayer do not need cheerful prayers who cannot be in silence themselves before the awful mystery of God. Entrance into a nursing home calls for massive reorganization of the self without many of the supports that hold one's self together, including the consolation of prayer. We have to be able to be with those who experience desolation or abandonment in silence. No word of consolation is appropriate; this is not a time of consolation. The struggle of the soul with God is intensely personal. Desolation may give way to a time of silence or quietness in prayer, to a new way of praying. To this we need to be attentive and supportive. (99)

Then, finally perhaps, the nursing home resident may come to new life. (99)

Is there anything we can do beforehand to prepare people for this time of life? In general it is important to speak forthrightly about the realities of life in the nursing home. Sensitive (and blunt) descriptions of the *spiritual* struggles of the new nursing home resident is a powerful way to expand the notion of the human and to help us rethink the sacredness of all life. There is much to teach and learn. What is required is that we bring back not simply cheerful messages (or worse, no messages at all), but stories of those often heroic struggles and successes in the life of the spirit—some of what they have learned about prayer, about life, about new identity, about new communication, about new friendship. (100-101)

Nursing home residents have much to teach us. If we are unafraid to draw close, we have much to learn and thus to preach. The lessons have a pointedness that gives new meaning to religious convictions that all life is holy and is part of God's gift. To speak of the giftedness of life is not to intimate that all life is equally friendly toward everyone. Sometimes as life passes on it doesn't seem to care much about some individuals. While life is gifted, it is also burdened by its fickleness. The nursing home resident who has learned anew to thank God for this life can be a powerful teacher and witness. (101)

GROUP DISCUSSION

PARTICIPANTS

8-10 educators, clergy, and congregants experienced in nursing home visitation

FORMAT

90 minutes; a continuing education event

OBJECTIVES

- To identify and prepare to meet specific spiritual needs of new nursing home residents
- To learn to listen for and share good news with residents

MATERIALS
- copies of Simmons'/Peters' article

PREPARATION
Arrange the room in a manner conducive to group discussion.

INSTRUCTIONS
1. Explain the process for the discussion: the leader will read Simmons'/Peters' article, pausing after each sentence; participants are free to comment, reflect aloud, or raise questions at any time. Proceed with the discussion. (50 minutes)
2. Form groups of 2-3. Ask the participants to discuss stories that nursing home residents have shared in which they learned about prayer, life, new identity, new communication, and new friendship. Ask the groups to formulate 1-2 strategies for sharing this good news in the congregation. (15 minutes).
3. Reassemble the large group. Have each small group share its stories and strategies. (15 minutes)
4. Invite the participants to a time of individual, quiet prayer. Dismiss the group with a benediction, and give each participant a copy of the selection from *With God's Oldest Friends*. (10 minutes).

Prayer: A Pathway for Spiritual Growth

READING

Using the burial service from the Book of Common Prayer *for structure, Edward Gleason examines the inevitable event of the death of a loved one. Actual stories are used to demonstrate that even through the pain of loss, survivors can reclaim life. The interweaving of liturgy and experience provides a rich texture for this book.*

Death happens, despite what we do to avoid it. Everything that begins ends. The fact may not be welcome, but it is realistic. Death is a central part of life, and despite everything it takes from us, so too it enriches and strengthens. (6)

Death may not happen every day, but many, many times in our lifetime. There is no other choice. When it happens, what do we say? Or think? To whom do we turn? What do we do? We have to do something. Is it just being there that matters most? That's a beginning. We feel useless. Death hurts. It really hurts. Make it go away. Why did this happen? There must be some mistake. (9)

No, there is no mistake. Death happens. When it happens, we join hands, literally and figuratively, with those whom we love, those who have loved us. Dumbstruck, struck down, we cannot just stand there, and so we bind ourselves to one another. (9)

God is made known in human life through the cross. We know God first through Jesus, whose cross is continually present in our daily experience. The cross of Jesus is every experience of death and loss, disappointment and defeat. (10)

Without death, there is no life, and so it is that in dying we live. (11)

Once we own up to death, grief is the process by which the losses of death are transformed into new life. It is a process we all frequently experience, every day and in small ways. It is an experience we have known from childhood. The experience is always unwelcome, but the process is consistent. Grief is the process by which loss is transformed into new life. (12)

When death happens, we join hands with those who know our pain most deeply. We meet them in many places, but when death happens, we have the opportunity to meet them first as the church, gathered together for the church's statement at the time of death, the Burial of the Dead in the *Book of Common Prayer*. Here we are united to our roots and the depths of our faith, gathered with those who love us, those alive and those long dead. Loss draws us into a band of friends, family, and lovers to face death with us and to surround us with a cloud of witnesses. In the center of that band, the cross proclaims, is Jesus the Christ, who died so that through death we might be given new life. (12)

Death is denied by our use of language, most especially in the frequent avoidance of the word itself. One does not die; one passes.

When life ends most persons speak not of death but of passing, as if death were not the dramatic end of life but merely a transition—a peaceful, pleasant passing. Death may sometimes be peaceful, but it is always a rupture, an ending, and it is unwelcome and painful. (26)

At the time of death we are laid bare. Nothing can be hidden, either from ourselves or from God. (55)

Loss is the prevailing and pervasive fact of human existence, but even in the midst of loss, especially in the midst of loss, God is present. Finally, there is no other source of help, none at all, save God. (60)

Death is inevitable, and we have the right and opportunity to meet it, face it, claim it, before it takes us. As Christians, we do so in the name and power and presence of Christ, the one who died so that we might live, the one who through baptism incorporates us into his death, so that we too shall partake of his resurrection. (84)

Resurrection means a new life, a life consistent with the past, but separate and different. Eternal life in baptism is new life, not more of the same old thing. Eternal life is different from immortality. (84)

When we sit in darkness and in the shadow of death, there are many people who have no knowledge of what that means. We want to sit with one who knows what it means to be in our kind of darkness, one who will lighten that darkness with a special understanding. Jesus is that person. (156)

The Lord will guide our feet into the way of peace, having taken away the sin of the world. (156)

He guides our feet into the way of peace with a presence that is first at one with us, but then apart from us; by Him we are made whole enough to live anew. (156)

MEMORIAL SERVICE

PARTICIPANTS

nursing home residents/staff, a hospice, chronic care hospital staff

FORMAT

a service to remember those who have died during the past year

OBJECTIVES
- To celebrate the lives of those who have died
- To recognize the loss those gathered are feeling because of the deaths that have touched them
- To affirm the new life offered by the resurrected Christ

MATERIALS
- large bowl of water
- cross (3 ft. x 4 ft.)
- colored markers
- white cloth
- candle
- matches
- copies of Gleason's article

PREPARATION

Arrange a circle of chairs and in the center place a large bowl of water on a table, along with a cross, a white cloth, colored markers, and an unlit candle. (If this service is held in a church, the participants might gather around the baptismal font.)

INSTRUCTIONS
1. Welcome those who have gathered. Ask them to name the people they wish to remember. Write the name of each person on the white cloth, using different colored inks. Place this "baptismal robe" on the table. (10-15 minutes)
2. Read from the Gleason article: "When death happens we are united to our roots and the depths of our faith, gathered with those who love us, those alive and those long dead. Loss draws us into a band of friends, family, and lovers to face death with us and to surround us with a cloud of witnesses. In the center of that band, the cross proclaims, is Jesus the Christ" (12). (10-15 minutes)
3. Invite the participants to sing the first verse of the hymn "For All the Saints," or read it as a prayer. (5 minutes)

4. Read each name written on the cloth, pausing after each name to invite the participants to tell something they remember about that person—a story, a treasured thought, a kindness done, a last meeting, etc. (30-40 minutes)

5. Read Revelation 21:10 and 21:22–22:5 twice, the second time pausing after each sentence for at least 30 seconds. At the words, "God's glory is its light, and its lamp is the Lamb," light the candle and pause again. At the words, "The angel showed me the river of the water of life . . ." scoop up the water in both hands and let it fall back into the basin. Do this 4-5 times. Pause again and then finish the reading. (20 minutes)

6. Offer a brief reflection, beginning with Gleason's words: "Resurrection means a new life, a life consistent with the past, but separate and different. Eternal life in baptism is new life, not more of the same old thing. Eternal life is different from immortality." The reflection should celebrate those who have died who made a difference by living out God's purpose for their lives. (10-15 minutes)

7. Dismiss with a prayer. Conclude with the following words, repeated by the participants: "We remember those who have died. We are united in mind and heart with family and friends, a cloud of faithful witness. We will not forget them. Nor will they ever be lost from God's loving memory. Amen." (15 minutes)

Community: A Pathway for Spiritual Growth

READING

Dayle A. Friedman writes out of her experience as a chaplain in a Jewish nursing home. Her fundamental convictions are that it is religious life that holds the promise of meaning, connection, and celebration for nursing home residents. Entering into the religious life of older adults in a nursing home is not only important for the community of faith, but also it is profoundly satisfying for those who engage in this ministry.

Being a nursing home resident is about being disconnected. You are cut off from the life you have lived until now and, often, from people and relationships that have nurtured you. When the staff members of the nursing home look at Mrs. S., they see a "pleasantly confused" and affable woman, not the president of the Hadassah chapter, who was legendary in her family for her noodle kugel and among her friends for her wry wit. Mr. G. was one of 12 children in a tightly knit family. Now he is alone, a "last twig," the sole survivor, whose only son lives in California and does what he can to stay in touch by phone and mail. (13)

In the nursing home you are in the midst of people—you share your room, your dining room table, and your "living room" with others, but they are not people you have chosen, and they may not be to your liking. So life in the nursing home can feel alienating indeed, and the institution's four walls can seem an impregnable barrier between it and the outside world. (13-14)

In our society the first question in social encounters is invariably "What do you do?" We measure worth by the productive labor in which we are engaged. We *are* what we do, so those who can no longer do the things they did over a lifetime—whether business or family nurturing or communal involvement—are robbed of a sense of their worth. So it is that Mrs. V., an 88-year-old nursing-home resident, says to me, "All my life I've done for others. I helped my mother, my husband, my niece and nephews. I worked for the synagogue and for organizations, and I gave to *tzedaka* every time I had a spare coin. Now I can't do anything for anyone. I can't walk, I can't see and I need help even to get dressed and to get out of bed. What good am I anymore? Why doesn't God just take me?" Along with the dependency and incapacity of nursing home residents comes a profound sense of uselessness and worthlessness. (14)

In contrast to the emptiness, disconnection, and uselessness that characterize life in the nursing home, I see the miraculous way in which Judaism gives older adults an opportunity to experience time as significant, to feel a sense of connection and to experience their own meaning. Simply put, I witness little miracles every day, for every day

I see how Jewish life manages to touch the part that is whole, even in broken-bodied and broken-minded people. (14)

Jewish life offers frail elders links to God, to the Jewish people and to one another, in dramatic contrast to the sense of disconnection so prevalent in the nursing home. (16)

One week, Freda has been suffering more than usual from her arthritis and needs to come to services in a wheelchair instead of with her customary walker. Because she has not found room in the aisle next to her friends, she has been placed behind the back pew. (16)

As I begin the service, I look up and notice that, without discussion, Bertha and Hannah have moved to the back pew, so that they can continue to sit with their friend despite her new physical limitation. (16)

This may be a nursing home, but these people are a community, and they offer one another love and support and companionship in the context of religious life. (16)

Mrs. V. and other residents wonder profoundly about their purpose in life. They feel they have nothing to give, no mission to accomplish. (16)

The Jewish tradition has a different message, however. As Jews, Mrs. V. and her fellow residents are participants in the covenant between God and the Jewish people. They are *metzuvim* (commanded persons), and as adult members of the community, they are obligated to serve God through performing the *mitzvot*, the ritual and ethical commandments given in the Torah. Obligation commences with *bar/bat mitzvah*, but it does not end with old age. There is neither retirement nor senior citizen discount from obligation. (16)

Thus, if Jews are called to a life of "Torah, worship, and acts of loving-kindness," then so, too, are my congregants. And if they are obligated, then they also have the opportunity to experience their own importance and power. (18)

The importance and power of these impaired, dependent, elderly Jews become apparent in their relationship with Yonah [an oppressed

Ethiopian Jew, whom they were trying to help as their *mitzvah* of fasting]. (18)

An Ethiopian Jewry committee was established in the nursing home. The residents "adopted" the family of Yonah Redday, a 26-year-old Ethiopian Jew, after hearing lectures on the plight of the 15,000 Jews left in Ethiopia. (18)

In their efforts to help Yonah, this young Jew halfway around the world, from a community that most of them had never heard of, my congregants were participants in the *mitzvah* of *pidyon shevuyim* (redeeming the captives). In Yonah's eyes, and in their own, they were no longer merely old people or sick people or recipients of care but redeemers whose prayers and wishes made a real difference in the life of this Jewish family. (18)

These events and others are the miracles of daily life in the nursing home. Through ritual, tradition, and community, individuals experience moments of celebration, connection, and meaning; their frailty and dependency are not erased, but they are joined by *kedushah* (holiness) and by dignity. I learn from my congregants not just the horrors of elderhood but the possibilities as well. (18)

Growing old is still a frightening prospect. But I can say I have learned from my tradition and from my elderly guides that amazing, magical, and miraculous things might just happen to me and to all of us when we get there. (18)

GROUP MINISTRY

PARTICIPANTS

minimum 4 people; a small group within the church that feels called to minister to those in long-term care facilities

FORMAT

2 sessions, 60 minutes each; a visit to the long-term care facility occurring between the sessions

OBJECTIVES
- To design a program of ministry for a particular long-term care facility
- To explore the expectations that members have for their work in a long-term care facility

MATERIALS
- newsprint
- markers
- copies of Friedman's article

PREPARATION
1. Distribute copies of the Friedman article to the participants.
2. Arrange a room conducive to group interaction.
3. Display the following quotes from the Friedman article in the room:

- "Being a nursing home resident is about being disconnected. You are cut off from the life you have lived until now and, often, from people and relationships that have nurtured you" (13).
- "Jewish life offers frail elders links to God, to the Jewish people, and to one another, in dramatic contrast to the sense of disconnection so prevalent in the nursing home" (16).
- "These events and others are the miracles of daily life in the nursing home. Through ritual, tradition, and community, individuals experience moments of celebration, connection, and meaning. Their frailty and dependency are not erased, but they are joined by kedushah (holiness) and by dignity. I learn from my congregants not just the horrors of elderhood but the possibilities as well" (18).

INSTRUCTIONS
Session 1
1. Begin with prayer. Then ask someone to read the quotes from the Friedman article. Ask for signs of agreement or disagreement by the show of hands. Then ask for reasons why the participants agree or disagree. (15 minutes)

2. If the group is large in number, form small groups of 3-4 each. Ask each group to appoint a member to record on newsprint results of their discussion. Have the participants brainstorm the challenges and promises they expect they will encounter in their ministry at a long-term care facility. (15 minutes)

3. Reassemble the large group. Ask the recorders to report on their group's findings. (10 minutes)

4. Summarize the ideas that have been presented. Ask the participants if their expectations are in keeping with the long-term care facility described by Friedman. Ask someone to record the results of the discussion on newsprint. (15 minutes)

5. Close by discussing the upcoming field trip. Ask a participant to close with prayer. (5 minutes)

Field Trip

Arrange with the administration of the long-term care facility at which the church's ministry will take place for a tour and orientation to the facility. At this time the participants in the ministry will meet the residents and staff, become familiar with the mission and philosophy of the long-term care facility, assess whether they are in keeping with the reality of the residents' daily lives, and hear from the residents about their daily lives—with its challenges and promise.

Session 2

1. Display the newsprint sheets from the first session. Begin with prayer. Briefly review what was discussed in the first session, using the newsprint sheets to guide your remarks. Remind the participants of Friedman's concern to give meaning to life in a nursing home. Then ask the participants for any impressions they wish to share from the field trip. Discuss any differences between the expectations raised in the first session and the reality of their field trip experience. (15 minutes)

2. Ask the participants to reassemble in the same small groups they were in during the first session. Bearing in mind the outcome of the first session's discussions and the field trip, have

each group brainstorm about the form and function their ministry might take in the long-term care facility. Remind the participants that the goal is a ministry *with*, not *to* those in the long-term care facility. Each group should appoint someone to record the ideas on newsprint. (20-25 minutes)

3. Reassemble the large group. Ask each group to report its ideas. Allow questions of clarification only. Have each group place its newsprint above that from the first session. Summarize the ideas presented, connecting similar ideas from the sessions. Check for accuracy with the group that originated the idea. (20 minutes)

4. If time allows, narrow the ideas presented into actual proposals for the form and function of the ministry. If time does not allow, schedule another session to initiate a preliminary plan—to be negotiated with those in the facility—for a ministry that will recognize, nourish, and facilitate connection, community, and links to the larger church. (5-10 minutes)

Source Notes

James L. Empereur, *Prophetic Anointing: God's Call to the Sick, the Elderly, and the Dying* (Wilmington DE: Michael Glazier, Inc., 1982). Used by permission of the author.

Joseph Folliet, *The Evening Sun: Growing Old Beautifully*, trans. D. Smith (Chicago: Franciscan Herald, 1983).

John LaFarge, *Reflections on Growing Old* (Chicago: Loyola University Press, 1963). Permission granted by the Provincial of the New York Province of the Society of Jesus.

Henry Simmons and Mark Peters, *With God's Oldest Friends: Pastoral Visiting in the Nursing Home* (Mahwah NJ: Paulist, 1996).

Copyright © 1990 by Edward Gleason. All rights reserved. Reprinted from *Dying We Live*, published by Cowley Publications, 28 Temple Place, Boston, MA 02111. (1- 800-225-1534)

Dayle A. Friedman, "Miracles Every Day: Jewish Life among the Old and Frail," *Brandeis Review* (Spring 1991). Reprinted from *Inside* (Winter 1991). Used by permission of the author.

chapter 6

DYING

Witness: A Pathway for Spiritual Growth

READING

From his candid admission that he has Parkinson's Disease to the essay's conclusion, John Yungblut shares a sensitive discussion of the many forms of diminishment we experience, including birth defects, natural disaster, unwilled separation, aging, and death. From his study of Teilhard de Chardin and his experience of contemplative prayer, he invites the reader into practices of mind, body, and soul that may help open us up to God.

I saw that the first step for me in learning to "hallow" the progressive diminishments in store for me was a deep-going acceptance. But the acceptance would have to be a positive, not a negative one, if it were to be a real hallowing. I must learn to do something creative with it. (6)

Treating one's diminishments as companions affords one a certain detachment from them that in turn allows one to exercise a kind of playfulness in relationship to them, to maintain a sense of humor about them. (6)

The forces of diminishments are not so much diminishments as deprivations from the beginning. Insofar as the person is conscious of these limitations it is a matter of creative acceptance, letting go of self-pity and bitterness. (8)

Bereavement caused by sudden accident often seems a greater tragedy than a protracted death through illness of the loved one. While a sudden death is a diminishment with reference to the unfulfilled life that might have been, the departed does not suffer the trauma of separation. This diminishment is borne by the survivors. (11)

The diminishments emanating from such sudden loss are terrible. Can such a diminishment be hallowed by any conceivable means? Yes, I believe it can in 4 ways. First, by daily committing the loved one into God's keeping, knowing that with God all things are well. Second, if there is an element of guilt in the suffering, by receiving and embracing forgiveness and living into the forgiven life. Third, by transferring to some other human need all the care and energy that had been consumed by the lost relationship—thereby realizing the phenomenon we referred to earlier that Charles Williams called substitution. And fourth, by growing in consciousness through these various processes so that one becomes more individuated, and thereby more sensitive to and available for the suffering of others. (11-12)

Hallowing the diminishment of bereavement or loss of a significant relationship demands both "letting go" of something that has been lost and embracing with enthusiasm something that has been found, or rather, given by grace. (13)

The experience of bereavement can take other forms of deprivation. It is not confined to loss of a particular person with whom one's life was deeply intertwined. Misfortune is versatile and performs its devastating vivisection on the psyche in other ways, too. (15)

Diminishments can take more subdued forms with the advancing years. For good counsel we cannot do better than to turn to Paul Tournier in his book, *Learn to Grow Old.* He speaks of the positive opportunities that retirement affords. There is always a certain diminishment one experiences in loss of persona. We may have identified ourselves too closely with our work persona, partly due to our need for self-esteem, partly because recognition is pleasant for us all, quite beyond the need of society to "place" us. (16)

If one is to hallow the diminishment of loss of persona, it is necessary to build a second career or to fill one's life with interesting, new, self-appointed work. Each of us must continue to exercise his or her gifts when the career of our middle years must end. (16-17)

The most effective workshop for learning how to hallow one's diminishments is the faithful practice of contemplative prayer. It is an art, a gentle art unique with each artist. It is an altered state of consciousness that comes only by grace, though one is called upon to dispose one's inner condition to be accessible to the gift that cannot be compelled. (24)

Contemplative prayer is a way of knowing one's self under the aspect of the eternal. It is the way to realize the ancient Gnostic wisdom contained in the words, "Whosoever knows oneself knows the All." We might also say, "Whosoever knows oneself as part of the All knows oneself and the All." This is the way par excellence of hallowing one's diminishments because one puts them in the keeping of the universe, "the way things are," so that while they have been lost to the ego they are not lost to the Self who is indistinguishable from the All or the One. At that moment, when one has finally let go of the diminishment, one is aware that nothing has been lost and that all is well. The diminishments have been hallowed. (24-25)

SERMON

TOPIC

"The Hallowing of Diminishment"

SCRIPTURE

John 21:15-19, used with the Yungblut article

FOCUS

Because Jesus knows us so totally, even in our losses and darkness, we can still support others in following Christ.

FUNCTION

To invite those who are unsure of their self-worth because they are no longer able themselves to follow Jesus and do his work.

THEME

The three segments of the Scripture reading are separate ("Do you love me . . ." "When you are old . . ." and "Follow me"). We begin with "When you are old . . ." The experience of having someone else dress you and take you where you don't want to go sums up many fears and realities of dependence in frail old age. It also reminds us of lesser but real diminishments that happen through-out life. When these diminishments occur, we become like Peter in the face of Jesus' threefold questioning of his love. We lose our old self-confidence and assertiveness. We hardly know if we have any love for God. We can only appeal to the Lord's totality of knowledge that includes the Lord's knowledge of our hearts.

We hear the words, "Feed my lambs/sheep," but we seem to have little left. In the sorrow of diminishments, what can we offer?

What Jesus asks of us now is simply to follow him, to go along with him on the way of the cross. We do not pray with the same confidence that we prayed with when we were strong. We con-template the cross and accept that nothing is lost to the One who knows us, loves us, and accepts our fragile love. It is enough.

Service: A Pathway for Spiritual Growth

READING

The mystical life goes through three stages or levels of spiritual growth. These stages include purgation (detachment from self-will and egocentric-ity), illumination (with the perception of God's presence in all things and the relationship of all things to God), and union (the permanent percep-tion of mystical experience). Wayne Teasdale joins this understanding to that of contemplation and the transformation of the earth.

Aging takes place in the perception of the knowing subject as well as in the body of the knower. It is thus a spiritual state as well as a physical fact. It is part of [a human's] self-understanding and one of the greatest challenges in life. (224)

Aging, in its ideal condition, is a progressive *clarification* of what life is. It is characterized by the enhancing of one's perspective on existence. For the process of aging—when the person is awake to its significance—is a *spiritual* phenomenon. It is growth in one's awareness of what is. Aging is also the environment of our search for the Absolute, the unfolding of the Mystery of life in our lives. It is also the revelation of the meaning of death, since all life—and aging as such—is a movement in relation to death and beyond. The Mystery of life, death, and eternity is not something the mind constructs, but is something objectively *meant* for consciousness. It is not subjective in origin, nor is it merely objective, since it engages consciousness. It is somehow tailor-made for us. (224)

Aging, as a process of striving to know and to live the Mystery of existence, takes its impulse primarily from the great puzzle of death. It is in this orientation that mystical wisdom is born. Wisdom is the insight into this question and its answer. Aging is the drama of living this answer. Socrates maintained that the whole point of life is to learn to die well, that life is a preparation for death, but that only he can die well who knows what life is all about. This knowledge is what constitutes wisdom. And this wisdom, "the pearl of great price," is essentially *mystical.* Thus, when life is lived in its depth, it is a process of spiritual growth, and aging is the medium through which this growth occurs. Aging is fulfilled in mystical awareness. This is wisdom in its profoundest sense, for true wisdom is the search for the Absolute, which is constitutional to human nature, and aging is the process of unfolding this search. (224)

In the modern world the elderly live in a state of spiritual deprivation. They are made to feel ashamed of their age. This is because the contemporary world does not live from a deep contact with the mystery of aging. Old people are alienated, because society values a productive function in its citizens rather than simply being a person. Function determines worth. The elderly who are not aware of their spiritual dimension tend to be lonely, bored, and lacking a sense of direction and self-worth. They consider themselves useless, as does society, because they cannot do something in the way of work. Since the modern world values *doing* rather than *being,* our elderly feel that their existence is devoid of purpose. Our world has lost its focus. It is out of touch with the meaning of being human. And it is because civilization has lost its spiritual focus that so many elderly lack such an awareness in their lives. They have become victims of a spiritually dull world, a world torn by violence, injustice, hatred, selfishness, and a monstrous indifference to the sufferings of others. Is it not possible to measure the moral and spiritual health of a society by the way it treats its older citizens? The world must regain its contact with the transcendent, with mystical wisdom, and rediscover the old ones as teachers of this wisdom. (224-25)

Aging—to apply the above—allows the forces of nature and grace to unite body and spirit in the expanded experience of living. As one lives and grows old, one actually experiences growth in the profoundest kind of knowledge, which is knowing *how to love*, and this is something only the Spirit can teach us. (232)

The "old ones," in the positive connotation of this term, are those who have confronted, understood, and accepted the fact of their aging. They are not running away from it. Why should they, since they realize that aging has an indisputable value? They perceive this value in a concrete sense of integration with the unfolding of their lives in the mystery of life's mystical or spiritual purpose. Those who have discovered this truth, and have allowed themselves to grow spiritually, age with extraordinary dignity and grace. Pope John XXIII, Mother Teresa, and Bede Griffiths are good examples of this attitude. The old ones are at peace within and with others, for they have found the source of happiness and genuine fulfillment in the mystical quest. And so they are joyful and full of hope. These men and women embody crucial values that are needed in the process of renewing the planet on all levels. These include: love, justice, peace, faith, unity, humanity, and solidarity with all living beings—to mention a few. (242)

The primary contribution that the elderly can make to every society and in every age is wisdom, mystical wisdom, which refocuses the value of life on what is ultimately essential for our happiness. As the aged recover the mystical sense, it will give them the necessary perspective and the vision to guide the rest of mankind in the historical reordering of the focus of value and motivation in society, away from an exclusive preoccupation with material ends—doing and having—to a new appreciation of our mystical vocation, which is the call to live in a state of permanent *intimacy* with God in the cave of the heart—the realm of *being*. It is the elderly, because of their wisdom, experience, and leisure, who can most of all cultivate the contemplative dimension. They can then share this precious wisdom with the younger generations and get them started on the mystical quest. (243)

My uncle, John Cosgrove, now in his early 80s and a beautiful example of that quality of *agedness*, a man of great spiritual wisdom, is fond of a saying that epitomizes what the elderly have to offer society, when he says: "Mysticism or contemplation is a treasure so difficult to find, and so easily lost if not worked at." Clearly, it is our collective and individual vocation to discover and cultivate the mystical garden within the cave of our own hearts. This is the entire significance of aging, as we are granted sufficient time to pursue it. In this regard, Thomas Keating has an important insight. Speaking to our contemplative depths, he says: "The greatest accomplishment in life is to be what we are, which is God's idea of what God wanted us to be when God brought us into being; and no idea of ours will ever change it. Accepting that gift is accepting God's will for us, and in its acceptance is found the path to growth and ultimate fulfillment." (247)

To be what we are, in the profoundest sense of Abbot Thomas' meaning, is achieved in its plenitude only in contemplative experience, in mystical life, in an enhanced identity found in that union with the Divine at the center of our own being. And so, aging is a spiritual process that finds completion in mystical consciousness, the progressive clarification of our being in God's. (247)

JOURNEY WITH DEATH

PARTICIPANTS

people who are dying and people who will accompany them on their journey to death

FORMAT

30-60 minutes with each willing participant; 60 minutes with those who will accompany the dying people; follow-up as the journey progresses

OBJECTIVES

- To allow dying people the gift of service to others
- To affirm the worth of dying people
- To expose others to the dying process

PREPARATION

1. Distribute copies of the Teasdale article to the participants.
2. Consider carefully who to involve in the project.

INSTRUCTIONS

Discuss the following points with each participant:

- The dying person has to know that he or she is free to say no. Henry once initiated a conversation with a long-time family friend who had cancer, asking her straightforwardly, "You're dying, aren't you, Lenore?" She said she was, and they spoke about it for a few moments, but then she said, "I'd like to be alone now." Some people will choose that path, and it must be clear that this is a deeply personal and legitimate choice.
- The dying person has to be reassured that he or she will set the boundaries that will shape the role of the companions on the journey, including the freedom to decide at some point that the journey is best undertaken alone or, at least, in shared silence. The minister should be prepared to facilitate this request.
- The dying person must be able to choose whom to invite. Companions can come from one's family or congregation. The minister should have specific congregants in mind—people who have already been approached (and, ideally, trained).
- Be aware that there may be someone absent whom the dying person would love to have present. Perhaps this is the person who doesn't come home or doesn't visit. The dying person's unfulfilled yearning can be a powerful force. At death, all relationships change. That process may begin as the person is dying.

- Monitor the process between the dying person and the companions. Be prepared to intervene if this seems advisable.

When all these conditions are met and the process goes forward, the dying person will be able to offer a great service; and those who share the journey will be enriched. Of course, after the person has died, the minister must meet with the companions to let them share their experiences.

Proclamation: A Pathway to Spiritual Growth

READING

Hershel Jonah Matt inquires about the relationship between the image of God and the human body (created in the image of God), as that body is observed to deteriorate. He affirms that no matter what stage of deterioration, the body is still the image of God. Finally, he affirms that there is a basis in traditional Jewish teaching for ultimate hope beyond the grave in the restoration of the soul to the body.

The creation of human beings in the divine image constitutes, as is well known, a primary affirmation of Jewish faith. It is primary in 2 senses: occurring as it does in the Torah's account of Creation, it is one of the very first affirmations; and, alluding as it does to the essential nature of human beings, it is one of the most basic. (75)

Normally, when we think of creation-in-the-image we assume—and when questioned, insist—that this refers not to any physical characteristics, but rather to our intellectual, rational, psychological or spiritual faculties. (75)

In an age that speaks so readily of "psychosomatic illness" and "holistic medicine," surely we should be able to understand what the ancients already sensed: that the image of God involves the whole person, body no less than soul. But to what extent does the divine image endure when there is serious weakening, malfunctioning, and deterioration of the body? (76-77)

What shall we say when deterioration has progressed to the point that the mind has *entirely* ceased to function, and such bodily functions as respiration and circulation and heartbeat and ingestion and digestion and elimination are sustained entirely through artificial means; when the patient, if disconnected, would immediately die? (78)

It almost seems that a human being, so completely dependent on machines, so fully interconnected, by pipes and tubes and wires, to multiple machines, has *become* a machine; that this "shell of a person," this "vegetable of a person"—what horrible expressions!—is no longer a person; that the image of God in this person has by now become so defaced that it has become completely effaced. (78-79)

Even in such a case, however, the aura of image persists. Our tradition, therefore, which requires us to show *kovod* (honor, respect, reverence) even for a corpse, would surely insist that greater *kavod* be shown to one who, however tenuously, still clings to life, to whom life still clings. Why is this so? Because however minimal the present level of functioning, this still-surviving human life can serve as a continuing, triple reminder: a reminder of this particular, formerly conscious and flourishing image of God; a reminder that in God's eyes the worth of a person *does not* depend—and in our eyes *should not* depend—on efficiency and utility or "quality" and normality; and a reminder of the abiding mystery of life, which extends from the very moment of its beginning (however indeterminable that exact moment is), when image is as yet only potentiality and anticipation, to the very moment of its ending (however indeterminable *that* exact moment is), when image now lies in retrospect and consummation. (79)

But even if there is debate, because there is uncertainty, as to when the exact moment of death occurs, one thing is certain: that moment eventually and inevitably arrives. Indeed, the very notion of life involves the notion of death (except, of course, for the eternally Living God): on the objective level, once life has begun, it has already begun moving toward its end; on the subjective level, once we become aware of the reality of any other person's death, we become aware of the possibility of our own—and, as we mature, aware also of its inevitability. (79)

Yes, the prospect of death, the eagerness for death, the fear of death, the denial of death—and, above all, the reality of death—are all present with special intensity in nursing home and hospital. Whether readily or reluctantly, whether immediately or only gradually, the realization comes that life has ceased to be; that creation has ended in destruction; that this particular image of God has completely faded out and disappeared. (80)

But though our body dies, is there not something about us—pleadingly we ask—that survives? Is there not some way in which the divine of us lives on? (80)

Biologically speaking, of course, we live on in our progeny, and this can be a source of comfort. That kind of survival, however, is for some of us too vague and impersonal, too "chemical"; besides, not all of us leave progeny. Whether or not we leave children behind, however, we all leave memories behind; in that sense, at least, we all live on—and this, too, can be a source of comfort. And yet our survivors' memories of us are almost sure to fade as time goes on; in any case, their memories of us will obviously die when they themselves die. Perhaps some of us can find some comfort in knowing that the influence of our words and deeds will continue on, directly or indirectly, even if we are no longer remembered or acknowledged as their source. For most of us, however, such survival is, once again, too general and diffuse to satisfy us. (81)

Is there no firm ground, then, in traditional Jewish teaching, for ultimate hope beyond the grave? There is. That hope lies in a double assurance: the assurance that each one of us lives on, even after death, in the enduring, caring memory of YHVH, who lives forever; and the assurance that YHVH, keeping faith with those who sleep in the dust, can be depended upon to restore us to life, body-soul life, in the Final Day—for judgment, reward-and-punishment, mending and purification, and life eternal. At moments of deepest faith and trust we rest secure in the divine assurance that the One who brought us into life by creating us in the divine image, who sustains us in life and eventually takes our life away, is not defeated by death but overcomes death in the Final Day. Then will the full measure of YHVH's power and justice and love be made manifest; each ailing, fading, disappearing image of God will then be healed, renewed, restored. (82)

SERMON

TOPIC

"Rabbi, the one you love is sick."

SCRIPTURE

John 11:1-45, used with the Matt article

FOCUS

Because God's love does not depend on the quality of human life, and because God's love promises a future beyond the grave, those who care for the most frail can be confident that their faithful care does God's work.

FUNCTION

To invite caregivers of the most frail in nursing homes and chronic care hospitals to celebrate their own caregiving in light of God's enduring, caring love.

THEME

As in the story of Lazarus, caregivers in nursing homes feel differently about the sick and dead. Some think how bad they stink—it is a hard job! Some see them as brothers or sisters they have come to love. Some believe that the Rabbi, Jesus, loves them deeply. Some believe that they will rise again on the last day. Some believe that the care they give is done for Jesus' sake.

Those who are frail remind us that the worth of a person does not depend on that person's quality of life; if a corpse should be treated with reverence and care, how much more carefully should those to whom life still clings be treated? Those who have died remind us of the double assurance that we will not be lost from the loving, caring memory of God, and that God who created us in the divine image is not defeated by death.

Those who care do God's work of showing love, whatever their personal faith. Like Mary in the story, who "anointed the feet of Jesus with perfume and dried his feet with her hair," caregivers do the most engaged and personal acts. In faith, we encourage them to celebrate how much they are signs of God's love, which never ends.

RITUAL

Express appreciation to the caregivers with a token and words: "My [sister/brother], your care for those whom God loves is a beautiful sign of that love. In their name and in ours, thank you."

Teaching: A Pathway to Spiritual Growth

READING

"To heal means to meet ourselves in a new way—in the newness of each moment where all is possible and nothing is limited to the old, our holdings released, our grasping seen with little surprise or judgment" (55). Stephen Levine suggests using meditation and visualization to accomplish the separation from one's body and mind and to think of suffering as part of the greater body or greater mind. If God can be seen in everything, then it is possible to start along the path of healing that becomes the path of life.

Along the path of healing that leads into the heart, one is often called upon to examine grief. Grief is the binding alloy of the armoring about the heart. Like a fire touched, the mind recoils at losing what it holds most dear. As the mind contracts about its grief, the spaciousness of the heart often seems very distant. (102)

Some believe they have no grief. This is another aspect of our rigid denial and self-protection. Some indeed may say, I haven't lost anyone—why should I be grieving? If only it were that simple. (102)

Most think of grief as a momentous sadness, but it is a lot subtler than that. Everyone has grief. Everyone seems to have some unbalanced tally sheet with life, some unfinished business. An incompleteness with the past and with ourselves, a fatiguing self-consciousness, the predominant theme of the unfinished symphony of mind's yearning. (102)

Our grief manifests as a self-judgment, as fear, as guilt, as anger and blame. It is that insistent mercilessness with ourselves and a world that we hardly let within. Our grief is our fear of loss, our fear of the unknown, our fear of death. Grief is the rope burns left behind when what we have held to most dearly is pulled out of reach, beyond our grasp. (102)

At the most microscopic level one sees that the tendency of the mind to hold, to cling and condemn, to judge, is an aspect of grief, a feeling of not-enoughness that longs to become otherwise. (102)

As we begin to direct the energy of forgiveness to ourselves and others, voices may arise that try to block that way of giving and receiving. These voices tell us that we are unworthy and useless. It is where we feel separate from ourselves, so many parts of mind pushed away, so little heart allowed to express itself. We wonder, looking into the warped mirror of our self-image, why what is reflected back seems so distorted, so unacceptable, so unwhole, and unlovable. (102-103)

But even grief is workable. Opening the heart to the mind's pain, we find space to explore mercifully. Then, instead of constantly appraising what looks back, we observe, we begin to look directly at what looks. We watch the watcher. We enter the eyes of discovery. And gently approaching the long-accumulated density of our grief, so long reacted to with aversion and disgust, we discover the unexplored territory between the heart and mind. And we acknowledge, with the sigh of letting go, how often we have distrusted what we feel. Examining what we feel, not analyzing why, we discover the labyrinthine patterns of our grief and unfinished business, the skeletons of so many moments of life that became lost by the wayside. And the darkness of a thousand moments of helplessness and hopelessness is illuminated in a clear and merciful awareness. That which has seemed so untouchable in the past is cradled in the arms of forgiveness and compassion, and the armoring begins to melt. The path to the heart becomes straight and clear, recognizing how this exploration of our grief, of the ways of our old suffering, opens the path to joy. Those who know their pain and their grief most intimately seem to be the lightest and most healed of the beings we have met. (103)

SMALL GROUP DISCUSSION

PARTICIPANTS

3-4 family members/friends of someone in the final stage of life, or volunteers who work with the dying, or someone who has just entered the dying process and is able and willing to participate

FORMAT

60-90 minutes per session

OBJECTIVES

- To provide examples of living people who have found healing through experiencing grief
- To learn the importance of creating a space to experience grief
- To point to paths of healing through grief

MATERIALS

- copies of Levine's article
- tape recorder or camcorder/appropriate tape (opt.)

PREPARATION

1. Distribute copies of the Levine article to the participants.
2. If possible, record the dying people telling their stories on audio or video tape.

INSTRUCTIONS

1. Welcome the participants. Introduce each exercise. Emphasize that the stories the participants are about to hear belong to someone, and therefore they may be discussed within the room only. (10 minutes)
2. Share the stories as told to you by the dying people or play their prerecorded tapes. Allow a time of silence between each story so that participants can react to what they have heard. After each story, have the participants articulate what they have learned about grief from the story. (30-35 minutes)
3. Ask the participants to think of ways they could use what they have learned from others to address the grief they are now experiencing. (15-20 minutes)
4. Dismiss the participants with a prayer that focuses on how they can learn about grief and healing from those who have struggled with it in the past and present. Ask for God's presence with all those who find themselves in the midst of grief. Petition Christ to secure a path for those who are grieving. Thank God for the gift of teachers such as those who are dying. (5-10 minutes)

5. Follow-up with the participants either individually or as a group to discuss any issues that the sessions raised.

Community: A Pathway to Spiritual Growth

READING

Using recent research and women's writings and experiences, Kathleen Fischer explores the themes of transitions, the inner life, contemplation, the body, mourning, remembering, caregiving, and intergenerational connections. Each chapter of her book ends with either a ritual, a prayer, or a meditation. These are interreligious and can be adapted or expanded by women in the later years or by those who work with them.

We think of wisdom as a gift of age. What is this elusive and mysterious quality? Observation tells us that it does not happen automatically; we can surely grow old without becoming wise. One element of wisdom is the accumulation of experience and the good judgment that results. But we hope for more—that as we age we will come closer to the very meaning of life. As women of wisdom, we return at last to the truth of our being, the ultimate mystery of the universe, the sacred dimension of existence. (64)

Mindfulness is both a spiritual practice and a way of being in the world. Simply put, it is learning to breathe slowly and fully while entering with joy into the present moment. It is a way to restore inner peace and in turn to be a part of the interwoven fabric of peace in the world. Part of the appeal of this spiritual path is that it can be practiced anywhere—while washing dishes, caring for someone who is ill, walking in the woods, lying in a hospital bed, driving the car. A key practice in learning mindfulness is to breathe consciously and slowly while repeating a *gatha*, or refrain. When we breathe consciously we learn to recognize breath as a contact point with the air around us and then with all life that has and will be on earth. There are many *gathas* [refrains], and their aim is to focus the mind and connect the simple with the profound. (68-69)

In centering prayer we quiet ourselves in a certain way to prepare for the disclosures of the divine image within. We wait in stillness for

God's coming. Since human powers have an innate tendency to scatter, it is necessary to center our energies in order to enter into this kind of vertical contemplation, which is sometimes called prayer of the heart. (72)

The goal of centering is to make God the center of our lives. We learn simply to *be* in the presence of God. Gradually this may open out into a sense of the oneness of all of creation: I am in God, and all that exists is in God. (72)

Women have never lived as long as we are living today. That means there are no established maps for the divine epiphanies we might encounter. In the middle and later decades we meet God in new ways. There are the agonizing losses and the unexpected graces, the things we thought we knew about God that disappear as life moves on, and the unfamiliar faces of the holy that appear in surprising places. There may be long periods when the God of our childhood disappears, leaving a vacancy that is not filled by any other belief. We become more aware of the depth and range of evil in the world, and try to reconcile our images of God with this consciousness. It is possible for our relationship with the divine to become an adventure filled with fresh revelations. (74)

God appeared to the Israelites wandering in the desert both in the darkness of the pillar of cloud and in the brightness of the pillar of fire. Our own path to the sacred may also be one of darkness, absence, and not knowing. Darkness is a dimension of all contemplation. For some, this darkness comes and goes; for others, it is the persistent path. In both instances, it can become a fruitful kind of darkness. (79)

Though darkness and emptiness in prayer can be sustaining experiences, it is important to recognize that for many women the sense of God's absence is painful and puzzling. We wonder if there is something the matter with us. We are angry at God or at the darkness. We fear it will never end. We feel guilty, and search to see what we have done to deserve this darkness. This is especially true if the darkness is a loss of a former way of knowing God. For example, a woman remembers how in her earlier years she rejoiced in God's felt presence and had it with her all the time. Then it was gone. She yearned for its return. She was frightened and felt she had lost her way. There seemed to be no one there to help; even the God on whom she had once relied was gone. (79-80)

As we age, it is important to realize that the many kinds of darkness we know can be opportunities for the deepening of love. Without such support and assurance, we will seek escape, suffer unnecessary pain, or fall into despair. For example, one kind of darkness that I have heard expressed by those in the last years of a long life is a sense of being abandoned by God. The light is dimming and going out, and they cannot find God's presence in the darkness. Older persons have expressed this to me in different ways, but one component is often a readiness to die and the inability to find any purpose for one's life. (81)

It is possible, on one level, to distinguish spiritual darkness from the darkness of depression and grief. Spiritual darkness is often accompanied by several signs: peace at a level deeper than the surface agitation and distress, a desire for spiritual experiences and a longing to pursue them even though usual forms no longer give satisfaction, and good functioning in the other areas of one's life. In other words, if we are maintaining work and relationships and wish to stay with this dry knowledge and awareness of God that does not satisfy the senses, then the combination of these 3 signs indicates life and growth. Such darkness in prayer does not incapacitate us. (82)

In the end, the same spiritual challenges exist in all kinds of darkness: to know that God is somehow present even when this is not apparent, to see the impasse as a call to new hope and vision, to find in the dying the paradoxical opportunities for life. (82)

Prayers that speak the language of the body are especially powerful when words alone no longer suffice. Some hospices give hand crosses to patients who wish them. These are plain wooden crosses that fit in the palm of the hand and can be gripped when someone is afraid or in pain. At such times, sensory identification with the sufferings of Jesus enables us to experience emotionally—not simply affirm intellectually—that another has known our fear of death, our treading of the winepress of suffering. In this mode of prayer we feel connected to another who understands; we are no longer alone. (92)

In the presence of bodily diminishment it is also helpful to pray in ways that focus not on what the body takes from us, but on what it continues to bring us. We turn from controlling the flesh to blessing our bodies for all that we have learned and can do because of them. (92)

RITUAL

PARTICIPANTS

a small group of which the dying individual has been a member, including the pastor and the primary caregiver

FORMAT

Recognizing that prayer changes through a person's life, the presentation of a handcross to someone in the final stage of life can be a meaningful way to acknowledge the gift of the here and now. It can be a powerful connection to a congregation that has been an important source of love and support for many years. Because of the individual's stage of life, it is unlikely that this ritual can be observed in the presence of the congregation.

OBJECTIVES

• To recognize the importance of prayer for those who are dying
• To provide for the dying person a symbol of life and suffering
• To demonstrate through the symbol that the dying person is the subject of the others' prayers

MATERIALS

• handcrosses

PREPARATION

Set up a space where the following ritual may be conducted.

INSTRUCTIONS

Follow this ritual outline: (15-30 minutes)

• *Sentences of Scripture*—Read the person's favorite Scripture or some verses from John (ex: 3:16; 11:25-26; 14:27) and the Old Testament (ex: Ps 46:1; Deut 33:27; Isa 41:10).
• *Presentation of the Handcross*—Present the handcross to the dying person. Explain that it is a gift from the congregation as a

symbol of continued love and support. Drawing on the Fischer article, explain that the cross can be used in prayer during times of peace or anguish to focus on God as the center of life, even when God seems absent.

- *Centering Prayer*—Explain this concept. If the individual has a *gatha* (refrain) he or she uses, employ it here. If not, suggest one such as "Holy God, be with me." Observe a period of silence.
- *Conclusion*—Conclude with a prayer that emphasizes the person belongs to God and is lifted to God by a loving congregation. Also allow the individual to pray.

Prayer: A Pathway to Spiritual Growth

READING

The "direct application of a mystical spirituality to the inevitable experience of death and dying . . . is first spirituality, and foremost spirituality as grace-in-crisis. Spirituality is, finally, life-in-the-midst-of-death" (xii). Employing the themes of Initiation: the mystery of death, Illumination: Nocturne, and Immolation: the sacrifice, Christopher Nugent weaves insights from 100 authors spanning centuries into a contemporary piece.

Glory is incandescent and ascensional, and we have tried to show that the dying of the light can be a dawning; requiem, a rainbow. (101)

Our recourse to a nocturnal theology was by no means to rejoice in some starless night, but to suggest that one cannot see the stars save by night. Nocturnal theology is a means to an end, and night herself is handmaiden of the light. (101)

In some sense this has been an essay on light and on love. Love is itself illuminative, and *if* in our climactic chapter we have taken it to its consummation (Greater love than this hath no one—John 15:13), let us now attempt to follow the light to its source. Let us honor our vocation to the light, to enlightenment, and not least "to the light of the world (John 8:12)." (101)

Light is a great miracle, and it can be seen as God's first gift (Gen 1:3), the primal sacrament. The gift is likely to be most cherished when, it would seem, least in supply—as with winter light, if you will. (102)

We are in peril of being spiritually blinded in a superfluity of artificial light. A world of cultivated, even boxed and packaged light, conditions us to be blind and "unironic" to the light that is residual in darkness and the darkness that is residual in our own light. We do not see the stars save by night, and we are unlikely to see them save removed from the cultivated light of the city. We cannot all reside in nature, but she is still our oldest resident teacher or, to be more precise, illustrator. And she is rich enough to provide reminders of the miracle of light in the wordless Magnificat of the late October leaves, simultaneously requiem and rainbow. Their very passage is praise. (103)

Death is ultimately too deep for tragedy, and let us return at last to the *Commedia* of Dante, the great poet of the light. If Dante takes us to hell and back, the *Paradiso* is suffused with light. His saints can be *hidden* in the light. All three parts of the *Commedia* end with the word stars (*stelle*), symbol of his hope. At first blinded by spiritual light, Dante climaxes in the Beatific Vision. Words fail, and Dante turns to the Trinitarian figure of threefold spheres of light, of rainbow from rainbow, weaving a celestial smile. Dante said: "I gazed." Who would not, for words are not equal to such wonderment? (103-104)

Dante gazed, and so should we. Done is our own nocturnal passage, illumined by the same Easter fire, and it is as dawn. May the wounded pilgrim be healed and any "midnight phantoms" vanquished by the ancient hymn to the victory of dawn, the *Aurora*, with which we prefaced our descent into the night. And may the turning to the light in dread, which began this essay, be a turning to the light in adoration, where it would end. (104)

At the beginning God said, "Let there be light." There was, and God saw that it was good. God gazed. This vision was the simple enjoyment of the truth, and, in the words of the Angelic Doctor, it was prayer. It was the first prayer. If we care, it is ours to end as on that first day of creation, with the primal prayer in the primal, and eternal, light. (104)

MEDITATION

PARTICIPANTS

   people who are dying, friends, relatives, fellow congregants

FORMAT

   Use the Nugent article as a meditation in any of the sessions on
   grief or loss, perhaps at the end when you wish to invite participants to embrace hope.

OBJECTIVES

   • To acknowledge that participants may find themselves in the
     darkness that comes when death is seen as an end
   • To guide the participants from the darkness of dying to the Light
     of God—the light of life eternal

MATERIALS

   • copies of Nugent's poem

INSTRUCTIONS

   Read the following text slowly, pausing after each phrase. You may
   wish to read it more than once, so that people who are dying and
   those who journey with them learn its rhythms, its hope, and its
   promise. (20-30 minutes)

   Glory is incandescent and ascensional
   The dying of the light can be a dawning
   Requiem, a rainbow.
   We do not rejoice in some starless night
   But suggest that one cannot see the stars save by night.
   Night herself is handmaiden of the light.
   Love is itself illuminative—
   Greater love than this has no one—
   Let us now attempt to follow the light to its source.
   Let us honor our vocation to the light,
   to enlightenment
   and not least to the light of the world.
   Light is a great miracle

God's first gift
the primal sacrament.
The gift is most likely to be most cherished when, it would
seem,
least in supply.
As with winter light.
We are in peril of being spiritually blinded
in a superfluity of artificial light,
a world of cultivated, even boxed and packaged light.
We do not see the stars save by night.
We cannot all reside in nature
but she is still our oldest resident teacher.
She is rich enough to provide reminders of the miracle of light
in the wordless Magnificat of the late October leaves,
simultaneously requiem and rainbow.
Their very passage is praise.
Death is ultimately too deep for tragedy.
Done is our nocturnal passage,
illumined by the same Easter fire,
and it is dawn.
May the wounded pilgrim be healed
and any midnight phantoms vanquished
by the ancient hymn to the victory of dawn.
And may the turning to the light in dread
be a turning to the light in adoration
where it would end.
At the beginning, God said,
Let there be light.
There was
and God saw it was good.
God gazed.
This vision was the simple enjoyment of the truth
and it was prayer.
It was the first prayer.

If we care, it is ours to end as on that first day of creation
with the primal prayer
in the primal
and eternal
light.

—Christopher Nugent

Source Notes

John Yungblut, PHP 292, *On Hallowing One's Diminishments* (Walling-ford PA: Pendle Hill Publications, 1990). Full pamphlet can be obtained by calling 1-800-742-3150.

Wayne Teasdale, "The Mystical Dimension of Aging," in *Aging: Spiritual Perspective*, ed. Francis V. Tiso (Lake Worth FL: Sunday Publications, 1982). Used by permission of the author.

Hershel Jonah Matt, "Fading Image of God? Theological Reflections of a Nursing Home Chaplain," in *Judaism: A Quarterly Journal of Jewish Life and Thought* 36/1, 1987.

From *Healing into Life and Death* by Stephen Levine, copyright © 1987 by Stephen Levine. Used by permission of Doubleday, a division of Random House, Inc.

Kathleen Fischer, *Autumn Gospel: Women in the Second Half of Life* (New York: Paulist, 1995).

Christopher Nugent, *Mysticism, Death, and Dying* (Albany NY: State University of New York Press, 1994). Reprinted by permission of the State University of New York Press ©1994, State University of New York.